TRADE UNIONS AND POLITICS
IN WESTERN EUROPE

TRADE UNIONS
AND POLITICS
IN
WESTERN EUROPE

Edited by
Jack Hayward

Professor of Politics, Hull University

FRANK CASS

First published 1980 in Great Britain by
FRANK CASS AND COMPANY LIMITED
Gainsborough House, Gainsborough Road,
London, E11 1RS, England

and in the United States of America by
FRANK CASS AND COMPANY LIMITED
c/o Biblio Distribution Centre
81 Adams Drive, P.O. Box 327, Totowa, N.J. 07511

British Library Cataloguing in Publication Data

Trade Unions and Politics in Western Europe
  1. Trade - unions - Europe - Political activity
  I. Hayward, Jack, *b. 1931*
  322'.3   HD8378

ISBN 0-7146-3155-8

This group of studies first appeared in a Special Issue
on 'Trade Unions and Politics in Western Europe' of
West European Politics, Vol. 3, No. 1, published by
Frank Cass & Co. Ltd.

Printed in Great Britain by
The Bourne Press, Bournemouth

Contents

Contents

Trade Union Movements and their Politico-Economic Environments: a Preliminary Framework

Jack Hayward*

The American political scientist V. O. Key has observed: "He who would understand politics in the large may ponder well the status of labor: a numerically great force in a society adhering to the doctine of the rule of numbers, yet without proportionate durable power as a class."[1] Despite the preoccupation with inordinate trade union power, which became a feature of public debate in some countries in the 1960s and 1970s, it remains generally true that the elites have been able to resist successfully the political and industrial challenges to their positions, even if significant concessions have sometimes had to be made. In Key's terms, the labour movement has not achieved either 'proportionate' or 'durable' power. To substantiate such a judgement cannot be the task of an exploratory exercise in defining the parameters of the discussion in a field where *parti pris* predominates. Part of the reason for the failure to achieve such power may be that it has usually not been perceived by trade unionists as the major objective. Trade unions have mainly been content to articulate the material demands of their members for a bigger share of the wealth produced by the capitalist system and to protect their jobs. It is the side effects of such action, in a highly interdependent economic system, that have provoked demands for legal constraints upon trade union power, rather than ambitious attempts by trade unions to displace the existing elites and abolish the capitalist system. However offensive to the politician and economic elites the piecemeal constraints imposed by trade unions upon their decision-making capacity have been, the defensive character of much trade union action should not be overlooked.

It is true, however, as was pointed out by both reactionary as well as revolutionary, religious as well as secular critics of industrial capitalism from the early nineteenth century, that the appeal to acquisitiveness—the insatiable demand for *more*—would undermine and eventually overwhelm traditional social restraints upon the inordinate appetite for wealth unleashed and legitimised by the Protestant Ethic. When the original restraint upon private appetite represented by the injunction to save and invest was replaced by the call to spend and consume, the explosive social and political implications of this commercial requirement were not grasped, despite the earlier warnings. As long as the mass of

* Professor of Politics, University of Hull; Visiting Professor at the University of Paris (*Sorbonne Nouvelle*), 1979-80.

the population had neither the will nor the capacity to act as 'economic men', with the uninhibited egotism characteristic of the industrial bourgeoisie, the jeremiads could be contemptuously dismissed. However, when the trade unions acquired the capacity to extort tribute from the employers to an extent that threatened their profitability at best and the very survival of their firms at worst; when the capacity of governments to contain the inflationary consequences of the mass of insatiable demands weakened; then calls to curb trade union freedom of action became increasingly vociferous. The disposition of trade unions un-inhibitedly to exploit their market power, coupled with the loss of legitimacy of the traditional social hierarchy and the increasing industrial and political strength of trade unions, have combined to challenge "the segregation of economy and polity so crucial to classical capitalism", necessitating "repeated political intervention, either to destroy the capacity to organize or to require the organized interest to operate through political rules".[2] So, like big business, the trade unions cannot be left simply to operate freely in the market and some accommodation must be reached with the state in a zero-sum game in which all cannot win.

If we are to distinguish between types of trade union movements according to their relationships with their politico-economic environ-ments, it would first appear to be desirable to clarify the variables differentiating trade union movements in terms of their ideological values, their organization, their representativeness and the techniques they use to attain their ends. Having established empirically what these characteristics of the trade union actors are in particular cultural and institutional contexts, it might then be possible (though it will not be attempted here) to see whether certain syndromes can be identified, prior to an examination of trade union relationships with employers (national and multinational), political parties, the political executive, the civil service and other public authorities, the judiciary, the mass media, public opinion and international trade union organizations.

Despite the fact that for most of their early history trade unions were treated as illegal restraints on trade in the labour market, there has been no general disposition in capitalist-pluralist systems on the part of the labour movement to abolish the market economy, either among the trade union leaders or the rank and file. Provided the limited objectives sought can be substantially attained within a market economy, the trade unions are content to work through this system, although it may have to be subjected to increasing state regulation and union pressure or even coercion in particular cases. In a country like Sweden, this seems clearly to be the case. However, where the market economy does not appear to be working successfully, public ownership may be adopted as a remedy, although this may be conceived in an *ad hoc* way and the firm or in-dustry may be managed upon market economy lines, which is the case in Britain. In other trade unions, e.g. the CFDT in France, a more in-transigently hostile attitude towards capitalism may be expressed, which demands a break with the existing way of owning and managing industry.

The leadership of this union, in its sixty year history, passed from an acquiescent attitude towards the capitalist market and the employer's untrammelled right to manage, to a root and branch rejection of this system, in terms of its values as well as of its everyday operation, in favour of self-management, via a phase in which it had placed its hopes in a democratically 'concerted economy' in which the trade unions would participate as full 'social partners'.[3] There is a wide range of types of 'industrial democracy', in some of which trade unions are designated as the agency of worker participation (as was envisaged by the 1977 Bullock Report in Britain), while the percentage of seats on the board reserved for worker directors envisaged or adopted have ranged from a small minority to parity with the employers. The central ideological issue raised by such practices is whether trade unions are engaged in class conflict or whether, despite conflicts of interest, it is possible to collaborate with employers (public or private) because of their partially common interests.

The extent to which trade unions are organized in a centralised or decentralised way depends in part upon the structure of the economy, as well as on the way in which employers' organizations and governments take their decisions. Furthermore, there may be a substantial difference between formal centralisation and actual decentralisation, notably in matters like pay bargaining. However, there tend to be fluctuations in this actual decentralisation as the 'two sides' perceive a negotiating advantage in concentrating their trial of strength sometimes at the summit and sometimes at lower levels down to the plant. Nevertheless, where the centre receives a large part of the union funds and where it controls the strike fund—which is the case in Sweden—we have indicators of de facto centralisation, while Britain has in theory and practice been highly decentralised.[4] Attempts at formulating a national incomes policy have often broken down in part because of the difficulty in reconciling the need for centralised summit negotiations with the reality of decentralised, shop-floor power. British experience provides an obvious illustration both of the short-term success of summit agreements and their medium-term failure, due to the de facto decentralisation of power within the British trade union movement.

A third important variable is the existence of either a united or a fragmented trade union movement, such fragmentation taking a number of different forms. Religion has been an important divisive factor, both in national and international trade union movements, although there has been a tendency towards de-confessionalisation, with class and status solidarity taking priority over religious affinity. Two Catholics one of whom is a worker, have less in common than two workers one of whom is a Catholic. However, in France, the de-confessionalisation of the CFTC was not achieved in 1964 without a split, with about 10 per cent of the membership retaining the old title—*Confédération Française des Travailleurs Chrétiens*—while the remainder adopted the new name of *Confédération Française Démocratique du Travail*. While religious divisions may represent in part a disguised form of political division, such splits may become overt, with Italy and France providing well documented examples of such fragmentation.[5] (We shall return to this point later in considering the relationship between trade unions and political parties.) Linguistic cleavages have also led to fragmentation, notably in Belgium, Spain and Switzerland. There are also sometimes divisions between craft and industrial unions, as well as between white-collar and staff unionism on the one hand and mainstream manual worker unionism on the other, arising from the desire to assert the separate identity of the skilled as against the unskilled or of lower-middle and middle-class unionism as against working-class unionism. Even when it has been possible to contain these fissiparous forces within one organization, such sources of disunity weaken the cohesion of the trade unions. Some 'yellow' or company unionism still exists but it is a relatively unimportant source of fragmentation.

Fourthly, union movements vary in their representativeness, as measured by the percentage of their potential constituency that they have been able to mobilize, either as paid up *members* or as *supporters* who will vote for union candidates or come out on strike when one has been called by the union. Although membership figures are often un-reliable and are therefore a less accurate measure of representativeness than they appear to be at first sight, there is a marked contrast between a country like Sweden, with nearly 90 per cent unionisation, and a country like France, with about 25 per cent unionisation. In between, Britain has a unionisation of 50 per cent, Italy of about 45 per cent, between 35 per cent and 40 per cent in Spain, while Federal Germany has some 39 per cent of its workforce unionised. Where, as in France and Federal Germany, there is a large-scale immigration of easily exploitable workers that are at the mercy of their employers in a way that indigenous labour is not, the trade union movement is weakened. Where the unions have been able to impose a 'closed shop' (which is the case for 5 million out of 12 million trade unionists in Britain) their representativeness increases immensely and with it their bargaining and coercive power.

Fifthly, unions vary a great deal in the extent to which they rely upon collective bargaining with employers and lobbying government and parliament on the one hand and upon strikes and various forms of direct action—including picketing and the occupation of the workplace—on the other hand. In countries with weak trade union movements or where the employers have resisted collective bargaining and the government has been unresponsive to lobbying, unions have been inclined to strike first and talk afterwards, when their reluctant interlocutors can perhaps be coerced into making concessions. In this matter of the means that should be used to attain their ends, union leaders are often out of step with their more militant members, who are less inclined to rely upon long-winded bargaining and lobbying methods and pay less attention to the constraints exacted by the economic circumstances prevailing at a particular time.

In turning to the relationships of trade unions to various factors in their environments, it is important to see such relationships not as unilateral attempts by, for example, governments to interfere with the unions or of unions to interfere with governments but as reciprocal parts of an interdependent but not harmonious whole. So, it is not possible to separate what is happening in the labour market from what happens within the political system. Of course, governments are now themselves major employers of labour, either directly or through various public agencies such as the nationalised industries. As such, they are in the position not merely of stating what is desirable in the matter of wages policy but of having to reach collective bargains with the trade unions in sectors for which they have direct responsibility. Furthermore, governments can modify the framework within which collective bargaining takes place through macro-economic policy decisions, notably in monetary, fiscal and employment matters and they may bring pressure to bear on private sector employers, e.g. through price control or public purchasing policy, to influence an apparently free process of collective bargaining. Governments may go further in a formal sense by statutory regulation through legislation, though such legal action may prove unenforceable in practice, both when applied directly to the trade unions or indirectly through the firms.

The relationship of trade unions to political parties has been an aspect of their overtly political role that has attracted the most attention. This relationship varies not only over time and space but as between central and local government (the combination of union and political office being more acceptable in the latter than in the former). There are four types of relationship. Firstly, there is the Leninist model, which has been more or (of late) less faithfully followed by Communists, in which the party, as the vanguard of the working class, dominates the trade union. Even when, as in the case of the PCF-dominated CGT, strenuous efforts are made to deny such party control and to assert the autonomy of trade unions, the precedence given to party over union interests is clear in terms of practical behaviour. Although attention is usually concentrated upon the overlap in membership at the top, it is even more significant that all the secretaries of the CGT *Unions départementales* and 90 per cent of the heads of its industrial federations are Communists.[6] Secondly and conversely, the trade union may be regarded as the vanguard of the working class as was the case with British Labourism. However, although the Labour Party was the offspring of the British trade union movement and remains closely bound to it in numerous ways, the relationship in Britain has evolved towards the third type, characteristic of Social Democratic party-trade union relationships in Scandinavia and the Federal German Republic, one of interdependence and symbiosis. In such a relationship, neither the political party nor the trade union movement enjoys an enduring dominant position; they see themselves as the political and industrial wings of a united working class movement, a unity not precluding frequent tactical and strategic conflicts. Finally, the trade union may seek to avoid any partisan affiliations. This may take the anarcho-syndicalist and militantly revolutionary form of the pre-First World War French CGT or the reformist shape of the post-

Second World War CGT-*Force Ouvrière,* content to improve the wages and conditions of its members by collective bargaining with employers or lobbying the government of whatever political hue. The bitter hostility of *Force Ouvrière* (as well as the other French unions) to crypto-corporatist attempts in the 1960s to convert the Economic and Social Council, in which trade unions are directly represented, into a second legislative Chamber by amalgamation with the Senate, makes clear that the commitment to independence of this type of trade unionism is not mere window-dressing. A similar hostility to any involvement with the French Common Programme of the Left from 1972 showed *Force Ouvrière's* capacity to resist blandishments from the Left as well as from the Right.

Two other aspects of the two-way trade union-political party relation merit some brief comment: the recruitment of personnel (members and leaders) and financial support (counterbalancing to varying degrees business support for Right-wing parties). In some countries, such as Britain and Germany, the trade union movement is a major source of party finance, whilst in others—Italy, Portugal and Spain—the unions depend on the parties for part of their financial support. In the case of Spain, the 'Socialist' trade union has also been helped with substantial 'loans' from the Swedish, Dutch, Belgian and (especially) German trade union movements, while both the Italian and Spanish trade unions are assisted by money received from emigrant workers. An interesting link between recruitment of leadership personnel and union finance in Spain is provided by the fact that those Socialist and Communist deputies and senators who combine parliamentary posts with their previous role as trade union officials contribute part of their salary to their trade union, whereas those who are not trade union officials contribute part of their salary to their political party.[7] The Spanish Communist Party has drawn heavily upon its trade union movement for activists, while the Spanish Socialist Party has continued to control its trade union movement despite formally forbidding in 1977 the combination of senior political and trade union office. In France, the CGT is an important source of recruitment for the PCF (which has strenuously resisted efforts to forbid the cumulation of party and union office) while the CFDT—especially from 1974-7 —has been an important source of PS activists. However, despite these links, there has been a variable tendency for the highly politicised unions in France, Italy and Spain to play their own autonomous role in the political economy, developing their own programme and choosing their own tactics.

While close links with a political party may secure for trade unions ministers who are themselves trade unionists or sympathetic to the trade unions, a situation characteristic of Britain, Federal Germany, Sweden and Switzerland, the trade unions usually do not have particularly good links with the civil service generally or even with their own sponsor ministry in particular. Ministries of Labour are notoriously weak, so even if the trade unions succeed in 'colonising' this department or its agencies, such action is seldom likely to enable the unions to dispense with using their "power to disrupt society" which Finer calls their *socio-economic leverage.*[8] In practice, trade unions may become partially incorporated into the administrative agencies with which they regularly deal and seek to shape the conduct of their members to accord with public policy. However, such developments are not likely to be immune from periodic eruptions of rank and file discontent and the reassertion of trade union autonomy. The fate of trade unionism in the USSR is a warning to any trade union leader who allows himself to become an extension of the state administrative apparatus. Trade union relations with public corporations, quangos and local authorities would also merit comparative investigation both within and between countries.

We have already alluded to the problem of legal regulation of trade unions, which is connected with the relations between trade unions and the judiciary. In contrast with France, where the weak unions regard labour law as a protection rather than a curb, in countries such as Britain where the unions have had to work within a legal framework (the English Common Law) that is systematically biased against them, the unions acquired an 'outlaw' mentality. They assumed that no good could be expected from the courts of law, so the unions sought to avoid becoming embroiled in legal disputes that would place them at the mercy of the judiciary. They accepted the privileged if precarious status of being a 'licensed conspiracy'. As the majority of the Donovan Commission expressed the traditional view a decade ago, "The British system of industrial relations is based on voluntarily agreed rules which, as a matter of principle, are not enforced by law. This is an outstanding characteristic which distinguishes it from the systems of many comparable countries".[9] However, as a member of this Royal Commission, Andrew Shonfield—inspired no doubt by his intimate knowledge of contrasting Continental European experience—put it in his 'Note of Reservation': "It seems inconceivable in the long run that in a society which is increasingly closely knit, where the provision of services to meet the elementary needs of civilised daily life depends more and more on the punctual performance of interrelated work tasks of a collective character, trade unions will be treated as if they had the right to be exempt from all but the most rudimentary legal obligations."[10] This debate has remained unresolved in Britain, with the union leaders wishing to be left free to manage discontent in their own way, the unions providing "the institutional channelling of animosity"[11] that may be regarded as usually supporting rather than threatening the status quo.

A more complete survey would involve touching on areas that have been neglected in this brief sketch, such as the attitude of public opinion and of the mass media towards trade unions and the reciprocal response of the latter to them. The mass media have played a notable part in whipping up a state of public hysteria in Britain about trade union domination which has been measured by opinion poll data,[12] while in Germany and Sweden business and Right-wing inspired polemics on the existence of a 'Trade Union State' have been given wide credence. Another aspect that would merit more thorough consideration is the international dimension of trade unionism, both in terms of the symmetry between the ideological and organizational division within national trade union movements where they are fragmented and the international alignment adopted when they are not, as well as the attempts to organize international union collaboration to co-ordinate pressure for common objectives, such as the thirty-five hour work week, both on states and on multinational corporations.[13] This partial reproduction at the international level of the conflicts at the national level will be explored more fully by later contributors, as will many of the other issues raised in this preliminary survey.

NOTES

1. V. O. Key, *Politics, Parties and Pressure Groups,* New York, Crowell, 3rd ed. 1953, p. 53.
2. Colin Crouch, 'Inflation and the political organisation of economic interests' in Fred Hirsch and John Goldthorpe (eds.), *The Political Economy of Inflation,* London, Martin Robertson, 1978, p. 220. See also J. Goldthorpe, *Ibid.* pp. 196 and 200-01.
3. See *La CFDT,* Paris, Eds. du Seuil, 1971 and Jack Hayward, "Dissentient France: the counter political culture', *West European Politics,* Vol. I, No. 3, Oct. 1978, pp. 59-62. See also F. Bloch-Lainé, *A la Recherche d'une 'Economie Concertée',* Paris, Eds. de L'Epargne, 1964.
4. Colin Crouch, *The Politics of Industrial Relations,* London, Fontana, 1979, pp. 26-7. See also Hugh Clegg, *Trade Unionism under Collective Bargaining,* Oxford, Basil Blackwell, 1976
5. See David Hine, 'The Labour Movement and Communism in France and Italy' in Martin Kolinsky and William Paterson (eds.), *Social and Political Movements in Western Europe,* London, Croom Helm, 1976, Ch. 7. See also the special issue on 'Trade Unions and Political Parties', *Government and Opposition,* XIII, No. 4, Autumn 1978.
6. Dominique Labbé, 'Les enjeux du 40e Congrès de la CGT', unpublished paper, ECPR workshop on Trade Unions and the Political System, Brussels, 1979, p.14.
7. Georges Couffignal, 'Les Syndicats Espagnols et l'élaboration d'un nouveau système politique', ECPR workshop, Brussels, 1979, pp. 8-12, 19.
8. S. E. Finer, 'The Political Power of Organized Labour', *Government and Opposition,* Vol. VIII, No. 4, Autumn 1973, p. 383.
9. Royal Commission on Trade Unions and Employers' Associations, 1965-1968, London, HMSO, Cmnd. 3623, 1968, p. 203.
10. *Ibid,* p. 289.
11. C. Wright Mills, *The New Men of Power,* 1948, p. 9, quoted in Richard Hyman, *Marxism and the Sociology of Trade Unionism,* London, Pluto Press, 1971, p. 37. On recent British experience, see Colin Crouch, *Class Conflict and the Industrial Relations Crisis, Compromise and Corporatism in the Policies of the British State,* London, Humanities Press, 1977, especially Part 3. More generally, see Colin Crouch and Alessandro Pizzorno (eds.), *The Resurgence of Class Conflict in Western Europe since 1968,* 2 vols., London, Macmillan, 1978.
12. See the 1963 and 1973 poll data reported in Jack Hayward, 'Royaume-Uni ou le consensus en crise', *Pouvoirs,* 1978, No. 5, pp. 145-7.

13. See Jacques Capdevielle and René Mouriaux, 'Structures syndicales européennes et Confédérations françaises: enjeux politiques intérieurs et internationaux', E.C.P.R. Workshop, Brussels, 1979, p. 9ff and René Mouriaux, 'La C.G.T. et les pays de l'Est—1947-1978', Centre d'études de la vie politique française contemporaine, Paris, 1978. More generally, see M. S. Joseph, 'Trade Unions in West European Politics' in Jack Hayward and R. N. Berkı (eds.), *State and Society in Contemporary Europe*, Oxford, Martin Robertson, 1979, pp. 86-90; cf. 243-4.

Trade Union Ideology and Workers' Conceptions of Class Inequality In France

Duncan Gallie*

A major difference between the French and the British trade unions lies in the nature of their ideologies and their typical modes of action. French unions place a strong emphasis on the need to sensitise workers to the exploitative nature of existing production relations and by extension to the fundamentally unjust character of capitalist society. British unions, on the other hand, typically conceive of their role as one of representing grievances and pushing for demands that are already consciously held by workers, and tend to reject the view that unions should actively seek to mould the way in which workers perceive the political and social organization of their society.[1] These differences in the goals of trade unionism are reflected in very different union strategies and modes of action on the shop floor, with the French unions placing a much greater stress on ideological contestation and issuing an incessant polemic against management and government through tracts and verbal persuasion. The explicit commitment of the French trade unions to the goal of raising class awareness poses the question of how successful they are in practice. Does the nature of trade union ideology and activity have a critical impact on the nature of working class attitudes to society?

Perhaps the most detailed and most convincing argument to the effect that the ideology of the French trade unions is of decisive importance for workers' social and political attitudes has been advanced by Richard Hamilton in *Affluence and the French Worker in the Fourth Republic.*[2] Hamilton set out to undermine the conventional wisdom of the theorists of industrialism of the late 1950s and early 1960s that the processes of social change in Western societies since the war were leading inexorably to the social integration of the working classes and thereby to the disappearance of major differences in levels of social radicalism between Western societies. In France, he argued, the decline in objective deprivations in workers' life situations was having no significant impact on the level of working class radicalism, and the critical reason for this he suggested was the nature of the French trade union movement. His grounds for assigning the trade unions such a privileged explanatory position are argued with a judicious mixture of common sense and theoretical acumen. Changes in objective life conditions he suggests have no inherent meaning; rather they are interpreted, they can be interpreted in different ways, and the critical agencies of interpretation are trade unions.[3]

* Reader in Sociology, University of Warwick

> The fact of rising or falling income, by itself, carries no political lesson. Any political significance, any lesson learned, is going to depend on the frame of reference of the individuals concerned . . . The frame of reference we are arguing, will depend on what the informal primary group leadership is teaching rather than on the "objective" facts of the case . . . For most people, without some leadership to show them, the link between economic events and the political sphere is so obscure that the question "who do we shoot" does not have a ready answer. (p. 6).

Given the salience of work in people's lives, it is the 'primary group leadership' at work that will be most critical for the way in which people interpret their experience, and the crucial leadership groups in the workplace are the trade unions. In France—at least in the larger and more modern firms—it is the CGT that defines reality:

> Post-war France and post-war Belgium both achieved sizeable increases in real income for manual workers; nevertheless the workers in one country remained persistently Communist and in the other persistently non-Communist. The difference is that in France the Communists won control of the most important trade unions in the immediate post-war years, while in Belgium the non-Communists scored the victory. In Belgium the new affluence is analyzed, interpreted and assessed by moderates; in France the same assessment is made for most workers by Communist militants. (p. 285)

It is important to note that Hamilton was not seeking to provide a general explanation of French working class radicalism.[4] Given the low levels of CGT membership within the French working class nationally (in the order of 25 per cent in the mid 1950s) it would have been implausible to argue that this could explain why more than 63 per cent of French workers 'sense much injustice', or why roughly half supported the French Left.[5] Rather, the core of his argument is that the role of the unions is crucial in the more modern, large-scale, firms that become increasingly characteristic of society as it industrialises. The paradox is that while more modern firms may have greater resources to take the edge off working-class deprivation, they at the same time provide the essential preconditions for effective union organization and hence make possible the propagation of counter-ideologies that can negate the effects of objective improvements in workers' conditions. The role of the unions is then destined to become *increasingly* important as the society develops a more advanced infrastructure.[6]

Given its potential theoretical importance, there has been surprisingly little attempt seriously to assess the hypothesis that union ideology is the critical determinant of worker attitudes to society. Yet despite the formidable barrage of tables with which Hamilton advances his thesis, the data he presents must—as he well realized—be seen as suggestive rather than as conclusive. He made imaginative use of three national opinion polls carried out in France in 1952, 1955 and 1956 respectively.[7] While these give valuable information about some aspects of worker attitudes at the time, they were in many ways ill-adapted to Hamilton's purposes.

First, none of the four key indicators of class radicalism that he deployed was entirely satisfactory. To tap the extent of diffuse class resentment, he relied on a question about whether or not people saw in the present state of affairs 'a lot of injustice or not much injustice'. The catch-all quality of the wording, that makes it perfectly legitimate for instance to answer in the affirmative while thinking about unjust pay differentials between *manual* workers, makes it difficult to assess its precision as an indicator of class resentment. A second measure related to whether or not people thought that social injustice would be improved by slow change or by revolution. Quite apart from the problem of whether or not this tells us if people actually thought revolution was desirable, the indicator was bedevilled by the fact that it was a follow-up question to the one on social injustice. As such, it inherited its problems and perhaps this explains why its effective response rate tumbled to 39 per cent.[8] A third crucial measure is one of Pro-Sovietism. The extent to which French workers regarded workers in the Soviet Union as being favourably or unfavourably placed was used as an indirect indicator of their attitude to the French Communist Party. This was ingenious and it had a much better response rate; it suffered from the disadvantages inherent in indirect measurement. Finally there was an indicator based on a question about workers' interest in worker movements in other regions and occupations, but this was used only sporadically in the analysis. In short, the initial portrait that Hamilton provides of worker radicalism is both lacking in depth and in precision.

The use of national samples also severely limited Hamilton's ability to look closely at the sectors of workers he was most interested in—those in relatively modern, large-scale enterprises that are likely to become increasingly typical in the future. Most of his critical attack focused on the implications of rising living standards and there was no analysis at all of the impact of technological change on either the experience of work or on workers' wider social attitudes. The data simply did not allow Hamilton to explore those sectors of industry which provided the most crucial test cases for his theoretical argument. Equally the use of sample data from just one country provided no adequate basis for assessing the distinctiveness of French workers and hence of knowing with any precision what *differences* in attitude one was setting out to explain by reference to the character of French trade unionism as contrasted with ideologically reformist trade unionism.

The research that would be needed to adequately substantiate or disconfirm Hamilton's thesis would need to be very extensive indeed. My intention here is not to try to foreclose what I would regard as one of the most important areas for further sociological investigation but rather to provide some additional data for discussion. This is drawn from a comparative study of workers in the highly automated oil-refining industry in France and Britain. The sample sizes (399 for France, 414 for Britain) do enable us to look more closely at the type of worker that is crucial to

Hamilton's thesis, and further its comparative nature gives us a better baseline for assessing the distinctiveness of French worker attitudes to class inequality. The interviews were carried out in 1971 and 1972 on random samples of operators and maintenance workers.[9]

CONCEPTIONS OF CLASS INEQUALITY

If Hamilton is correct about the decisive importance of the character of the trade union movement, then workers in similar situations of relative affluence and employment in a technologically advanced industry should be characterised by profoundly different attitudes in societies with different forms of trade unionism. Our first objective must be to assess the extent to which this is the case. In order to make any serious evaluation of the workers' radicalism we need data on four conceptually distinct elements of their attitudes to class inequality: its salience, the extent to which it is regarded as legitimate, the degree to which it is thought to be sustained by political mechanisms, and finally people's beliefs about whether or not it is transformable through purposive political action.[10]

How salient was the experience of class inequality? We investigated this by asking people whether they felt that they had disadvantages in their lives because they were manual workers. Our aim was to discover whether or not people felt that their class situation significantly affected the overall quality of their lives.[11] In practice we found that there was a marked difference in the importance attributed to class position by French and British workers. Less than a quarter (24 per cent) of the British thought that manual workers suffered from any marked degree of disadvantage because they were manual workers. In France on the other hand over half of the workers interviewed (58 per cent) felt a fairly sharp sense of class deprivation (see Table 1). Although our measure was a different one, the data confirm earlier findings in British research about the low salience of class inequality. Both Runciman and Scase[12] have noted the relative rareness with which workers make comparisons with non-manual reference groups. British workers tend to compare their fortunes with those of other workers and are relatively unconcerned about the wider inequalities between social classes.

The fact that class inequality is not salient to people does not, of course, mean that they are oblivious of the fact that there are wide differences in income, status and power between people in different socioeconomic groups or that they have no conception of society as class divided. Over 90 per cent of workers in both countries were able to give some type of description of the class structure, and equally over 90 per cent of workers—when directly asked—thought that there was either a great deal or quite a lot of difference between the standard of living of businessmen or members of the liberal professions and that of manual workers.[13] The British workers, then, were fully aware of the existence of inequality, but they were less likely than the French to believe that these inequalities made a great deal of difference to the quality of life.

TABLE 1

ATTITUDES TO INEQUALITY OF FRENCH AND BRITISH WORKERS

	French %	British %
Disadvantages in Life of Being a Worker		
A lot / Quite a few	58	24
Few	24	48
None	18	28
	(N=398)	(N=414)
Differences in Standard of living		
between businessmen and workers		
A big difference	74	60
Quite big	23	32
Small/None	3	8
	(N=399)	(N=413)
Legitimacy of differences in		
standard of living		
Completely just	10	46
Should be less great	60	38
Should be much less great/no difference	30	16
	(N=399)	(N=412)
Influence of Big Business over		
major political decision		
Greater than that of unions	71	45
The same	24	43
Less great	5	12
	(N=388)	(N=401)
Taxation system is		
Just	6	29
Not very just	33	30
Rather unjust	22	23
Very unjust	40	19
	(N=399)	(N=414)
% giving discrimination in favour of rich as first		
criticism of the taxation system	50	21
	(N=374)	(N=292)
Methods of Reducing Inequality		
A government more favourable to workers	39	14
Changes in the Constitution	14	10
'Naturally' through economic growth	17	37
'It will always be much the same'	30	40
	(N=381)	(N=407)

Independently of the importance that was attributed to class inequality as a factor determining the character of their lives, to what extent did workers in the two countries regard existing differentials as legitimate? For both French and British workers, the single most important source of differentiation between the classes was thought to be money.[14] This was mentioned more than twice as frequently as any other factor. To assess the legitimacy of existing financial differentials, we followed up the question of whether people thought that there were substantial differences in the standard of living of businessmen and professionals on the one hand, and of manual workers on the other, by asking people whether they considered such differences to be just, or that they should be less great.[15] British workers were notably more likely to feel that existing differences were legitimate: nearly half (46 per cent) thought that such inter-class financial differences were just, and the great majority of those who believed that society should be more egalitarian seemed to conceive of this in terms of a fairly moderate degree of change. In France, workers who regarded inter-class financial differences as just amounted to no more than 10 per cent in all. Moreover, nearly a third (31 per cent) of French workers appeared to be thinking in terms of a fairly substantial modification of the existing pattern of differentials. The French, then, were both more likely to feel that class position affected the overall quality of life and were more radical in the type of change that they believed would be required to meet the criterion of social justice. However, it is clear that the low salience of class inequality to British workers cannot be explained purely in terms of moral commitment to the norms governing the existing allocation of resources. The British were certainly more likely to accept the fairness of the status quo, but a majority, albeit a small one, would nonetheless have preferred greater equality.

A central component of most definitions of class radicalism is that workers should perceive an interconnection between class inequality and the prevailing structure of political power.[16] One approach to this is to examine whether people feel that there is an imbalance in the political influence that is wielded by the respective class organizations of big business and the trade unions. We asked workers in both countries to rank the influence of big business and the unions over major political decisions on a scale that ran from very great to very small.[17] If we take first the British case, we find that a majority of workers did not believe that business influence over political decisions was greater than that of the unions. But the majority is a small one (55 per cent) and the British are best characterised as highly divided in their assessment of the balance of class power at the political level. In contrast, the great majority of French workers were agreed about the supremacy of business interests in the political arena—with 71 per cent believing that business power was dominant. This difference in the assessment of class political power cannot be explained in terms of the prevailing type of government. At the time of the interviews, there were right-wing governments in both countries. Rather the data seemed to indicate a difference in the underlying conception of the role of the state. For British workers, state action appears to have been viewed by a majority of workers as impartial or 'neutral' in its reflection of class interests *even* in a period of right-wing government, whereas in France the state was seen as reflecting decisively the interests of big business.

This difference in the perceived 'neutrality' of the state for the question of class inequality is confirmed if we look at the markedly different attitudes of French and British workers to the fiscal system. Dissatisfaction with the taxation system was very widespread in both countries, with only 29 per cent of the British and as few as 6 per cent of French workers thinking that it was just.[18] Indeed 41 per cent of British workers and 62 per cent of the French took the more extreme options and considered the system either rather or very unjust. However, the sources of discontent in the two countries appear to have been very different. In Britain when people were asked why they felt that the system was unjust the most frequent reply—given by 46 per cent of British workers —was quite simply that taxation was too heavy and this resentment appears to have been particularly strong in connection with the taxing of overtime work. In France, on the other hand, criticism was predominantly directed at the way in which the taxation system favoured the rich and hit the poor. 50 per cent of French workers gave this as their first point of criticism while no other source of dissatisfaction was given by as much as 10 per cent of the workforce. The French were more than twice as likely as the British (21 per cent) to give inter-class criticism of the fiscal system. In France, through its control of the fiscal system, the state was seen as playing a direct role in sustaining the structure of class inequality. In Britain, although the workers were highly critical of the tax system, they did not appear to regard it as a significant factor contributing to the persistence of class inequality. Again, the British appeared to see the activities of the state in essentially 'neutral' terms, whereas the French viewed them as reflecting the interests of the more privileged economic groups in society.

Finally, did people look on class inequality fatalistically or did they believe that it could be transformed through purposive social action? In the case of British workers, Goldthorpe et al have stressed the extent to which class inequality was seen as a necessary feature of society, either because it was thought to derive from innate differences in ability or because it was thought to be essential if there were to be adequate incentives to motivate people.[19] Clearly where beliefs of this type are prevalent projects for radical social change are unlikely to find fertile ground however much workers are aware of the disadvantages inherent in their class position.

In asking people 'what do you think is the best way of trying to reduce inequality in society?', we gave two options that focused on political means of change: either through trying to get a government more favourable to workers or, more radically, through changing the existing constitution. In addition there were two options of a more deterministic kind. The first suggested that inequality would be reduced 'naturally' as the country grew richer, and the second was drastically fatalistic: 'I think there is very little that one can do about inequality. It will always be much the same'.[20]

Just as Goldthorpe et al had found, the typical response among British workers was deterministic in type and played down the possibility of introducing radical change through political action. Indeed, the single most common response was that 'it will always be much the same' and this was given by 40 per cent of the British workers. Insofar as the British did believe that there was a long-term possibility for greater social equality this was thought to be a natural outcome of economic growth. However—in both cases—the tendency is to see social inequality as the product of largely impersonal forces and hence as unamenable to purposive efforts to bring about change. In sharp contrast, a majority of French workers chose 'voluntarist' options and affirmed the efficacy of political action. This was the case with 52 per cent of the French as compared to only 23 per cent of the British. However, a reduction in social inequality was not seen by most as requiring a revolutionary up-heaval in the structure of the political institutions themselves. Only 14 per cent of French workers thought it would be necessary to change the existing constitution whereas 39 per cent believed that the principal pre-requisite for social change was that a government should be elected that would be concerned to forward the interests of the working class. At least in their attitudes to the political institutions, these French workers would appear to have been 'reformist' rather than 'revolutionary'.

By and large, then, Hamilton's argument that major differences would persist between capitalist societies in workers' reaction to inequality despite a broadly similar decline in several of the types of deprivation characteristic of the pre-war period appears to be amply confirmed by this data. In a similarly advantageous position both in terms of income and work task, French and British workers prove to have very different attitudes to their societies. The French regarded class inequality as more central to the quality of life, they were more dissatisfied with inter-class differences in the standard of living, they were more likely to believe that there was an important connection between the persistence of in-equality and the activities of the state and finally they were more likely to believe that class inequality could be reduced through political action and they were less likely to see it as the product of impersonal social forces. However, if we conclude that Hamilton is correct descriptively in that major differences in social attitudes do persist in advanced Western societies, how strong is the evidence for his argument that the explana-tion for this is to be found in the way in which trade unions interpret social reality for workers?

THE DIRECT IDEOLOGICAL INFLUENCE OF THE UNIONS

We can deal very briefly with the British case. The thesis as formulated would not lead us to expect that the type of union to which workers belonged in Britain would have any major implications for their attitudes to class inequality. While British unions do differ in their views about stratification *within* the working class, they do not appear to differ in any systematic way in their degree of commitment to structural change in the wider society. In comparison to the French unions, they would appear to be grouped at a very similar point on the ideological spectrum and to be fundamentally 'reformist' in terms of their longer-term objectives.

The situation should, of course, be radically different in France. Here, there is a much wider range of union ideology, and on the basis of the theory, as it has been presented by Hamilton, we would expect that differential exposure to specific union ideologies would have a marked impact on the way in which people perceive their society. There were, in fact, three major unions in the French factories—the CGT (*Confédéra-*

tion Générale du Travail), the CFDT (*Confédération Démocratique du Travail*) and FO (*Force Ouvrière*). The CGT and the CFDT are the clearest examples of unions of mobilisation actively seeking to develop a consciousness of exploitation in the working class. *Force Ouvrière* was much nearer to the conception of unionism typical of the British unions: it emphasised the value of negotiation and partial reform as against what it regarded as the millenarian perspectives of its rivals.

French workers, then, were exposed to a range of rather different views about what they should be thinking and at times inter-union disagreement reached a startling degree of ferocity. The CGT had achieved a dominant position within both of our factories, as it had nationally among unionized workers in France. In terms of numerical strength, it was followed respectively by the CFDT and FO. In contrast to the British situation, a significant proportion of workers (17 per cent) remained outside any union organisation and indeed the non-unionized in our factories were the largest single block of workers after the CGT members. However, by French standards the level of unionism was high—83 per cent—whereas the national figure for manual workers is in the region of 32 per cent. In part, this reflected the fact that they were employed in relatively large-scale factories. The level of union membership is markedly higher in factories with more than 500 workers and in factories of a similar size to our own there would appear to be an average union density of over 50 per cent.[21]

It possibly also reflects the greater stability of employment associated with continuous-process production, a stability which may be becoming increasingly typical of large scale firms.[22] A relatively high level of unionism was also evident in the British factories which operated an effective closed shop, whereas nationally only some 50 per cent of manual workers in the private sector are union members. This is of course very much as Hamilton predicted: economic development would bring about increases in plant size and thereby facilitate the growth of union recruitment and the concomitant exposure of workers to union ideology.

If Hamilton is correct that the activists of an individual's union act as an informal primary group leadership which 'teaches' the members a specific interpretation of the objective facts, then we should expect to find a substantial variation in attitude between on the one hand members of the most powerful unions of mobilisation (the CGT and the CFDT) and on the other, of non-union members or members of a reformist union such as *Force Ouvrière*. If we look first at CGT members, there would appear to be ground for suspecting that exposure to union ideology has some degree of influence. CGT members are systematically more radical than the non-unionized or members of *Force Ouvrière* (Table 2). However, the differences tend to be fairly modest and the degree of influence of union membership varies significantly depending on the particular aspect of people's conceptions of inequality under consideration.

CGT members were some 10 per cent more likely than the non-

TABLE 2

ATTITUDES TO INEQUALITY AMONG FRENCH WORKERS BY UNION

	Non-Unionized %	FO %	CFDT %	CGT %
Disadvantages in Life of Being a Worker				
A lot/Quite a few	52	50	51	62
	(N=67)	(N=22)	(N=51)	(N=253)
Differences in Standard of Living between businessmen and workers				
A big difference	59	86	82	76
	(N=68)	(N=22)	(N=51)	(N=253)
Legitimacy of differences in standard of living				
Should be less great	65	64	67	57
Should be much less great/no difference	21	32	20	36
	(N=68)	(N=22)	(N=51)	(N=253)
Influence of Big Business over major political decisions				
Greater than that of the unions	60	77	78	73
	(N=63)	(N=22)	(N=50)	(N=249)
Taxation system is				
Rather unjust	24	32	26	20
Very unjust	28	32	26	47
	(N=68)	(N=22)	(N=51)	(N=253)
% giving discrimination in favour of the rich as first criticism of tax system	34	48	67	50
	(N=64)	(N=21)	(N=49)	(N=241)
Methods of Reducing Inequality				
A government more favourable to workers	41	35	34	40
Changes in the constitution	9	15	14	15
	(N=64)	(N=20)	(N=50)	(N=243)

Note: The Ns for this table refer to the overall number of respondents answering this question for each column.

unionized to feel that their class position had major consequences for the quality of their lives. This is not negligible but it should be noted that not only do a majority of non-unionized (52 per cent) regard class inequality as salient in their lives but that French workers who are *not* in unions are still approximately twice as likely as British workers who are in unions to think that this is the case. The main areas of distinctiveness of the CGT members concern their notably stronger feeling that inequalities in living standards between classes should be reduced and in their higher level of resentment about the unjust character of the taxation system. Indeed some 47 per cent of the CGT members thought that the fiscal system was very unjust—compared to 28 per cent of the non-unionized and 32 per cent of *Force Ouvrière* members. However, it appears that exposure to CGT doctrine has relatively little effect on whether or not workers believe that inequality can be reduced through intentional political action. The relatively high level of belief in the possibility of political intervention in comparison to the British workers characterizes both the unionized and the non-unionized French workers.

If we turn our attention to the CFDT, the evidence for the impact of union ideology is almost negligible. CFDT workers are marginally *less* likely than non-unionized workers to believe that their class situation has a major impact on their lives and they are virtually identical to the non-unionized in their views about the extent to which present income differentials should be reduced. This is altogether remarkable given the fact that one of the most characteristic features of the CFDT's doctrinal efforts is its sustained assault on existing financial differentials. Similarly, CFDT adherents are if anything less radical in their views about the taxation system and about the possibility of introducing fundamental change in class inequality through political means. Indeed, overall, the CFDT members would appear to be the least radical of the groups under consideration.

It could be objected that by focusing primarily on political mechanisms for the reduction of inequality our questions fail to tap the most distinctive areas of CFDT radicalism. While accepting that political action is important, the CFDT has differed from the CGT in laying a much greater stress on the importance for any effective transformation of class inequality of a much wider restructuring of power relations in society, the key element of which would be the abolition of existing institutional hierarchies and their replacement by new forms of organization based on self-government. Possibly, then, by not providing for the scenario most closely associated with the CFDT we have underestimated the efficacy of its propaganda.

We can check whether or not this is the case by examining the way the CFDT members responded to a question explicitly focusing on the type of management of the firm that they regarded as most satisfactory. The question is a pretty crude one, but it gives us a rough indication of the types of project for change that workers were willing to endorse. People were asked whether they would prefer the firm that they worked for to be run by the State, by the unions, by the whole personnel or as it was at present (Table 3).

TABLE 3
ATTITUDES TO CONTROL OF THE ENTERPRISE
AMONG FRENCH WORKERS BY UNION

	Non-Unionized	FO	CFDT	CGT
	%	%	%	%
It should be run:				
By the state	8	9	8	12
By the unions	2	5	2	12
By the whole personnel	18	23	21	24
As it is	73	64	69	53
	(N=66)	(N=22)	(N=48)	(N=233)

Inspection of the data suggests it is unlikely that the earlier evidence indicating relatively low levels of radicalism among CFDT members was an artifact of the questions used. Of workers affiliated to trade unions, CFDT members were by far the most likely to consider that it was best to keep to the existing system. If we look at the option that accords most closely with official CFDT goals—that the firm should be run by the whole personnel—the CFDT members are the least likely to give it as their preference. Parenthetically, we can note that the answers to this question reveal that the CGT had also been largely unsuccessful in winning any widespread degree of commitment to its own objective for change in the economic structure—the nationalisation of the means of production.

This question was borrowed from a wider study of the French working class by Adam *et al.* conducted in 1969.[23] If we return to the original data it is clear that our own findings are not particularly idiosyncratic in their picture of the influence of CFDT ideology. Members of *Force Ouvrière* are notably more likely than CFDT workers to support the idea of self-government in the firm and in general there is virtually no systematic relationship between the preferred formulas for change of the official union leaderships and those that had currency among their respective memberships.

In short, if in general the data for the CGT do support the idea that unionism of mobilisation can have a certain degree of influence on workers' attitudes to social inequality, the evidence for the CFDT fails hopelessly to fit the hypothesis. The difference between the influence on attitudes of the two organizations may partly reflect differences in the efficiency with which union propaganda is formulated and distributed or it may show that it is only in the long term that union agitation can have any impact. It is only since the mid-60s that the CFDT has adopted a radical posture with regard to class inequality and presumably it was not an easy move for its membership to carry out such a radical ideological conversion after years of assimilation of a more conservative doctrine heavily marked by the Catholic principle of the ideal of social harmony.

However, even the data for the CGT indicate that union influence at best is rather weak, and this raises the question of why this should be the case. One answer might be that a comparison of union members and non-members in factories in which the unions are active is a misleading test of the net effect of exposure to union ideology. While it fits the demands of a theory pivoted on the assumption of the central importance of tested opinion leaders, arguably there might be an important spill-over effect in which non-members might be influenced by union ideas, thus decreasing the difference between their own positions and those of the unionized. This hypothesis cannot, of course, be tested directly with our own data, but it is an argument that Hamilton himself examined, using his wider data on the French working class, *and rejected*. What emerges clearly from his analysis is that when non-unionized workers are compared in situations in which unions are very active, inactive and non-existent, there is very little difference in their social attitudes. In so far as there was a difference, the non-unionized were actually *less* radical where the unions were very active than where they were non-existent. Hamilton comments: 'The non-members in active union plants are not especially swayed in the direction of increased radicalism or increased class consciousness . . . This indicates that non-members in active union firms have managed somehow to avoid the union pressure and influences'.[24]

Similarly, the density of union membership in our factories does not seem to have been particularly crucial. The precious little national data that we have on these questions reveals the influence of union ideology as every bit as weak. For instance, the 1967 French national election study asked people whether and how strongly they agreed with the statement that 'in the distribution of national revenue, the workers were disadvantaged'. This relates fairly closely to our question about the legitimacy of differentials in the standard of living. If we examine the distribution of answers among the French male manual workers, we find that 68 per cent of CGT members strongly agreed that this was the case, whereas this was true for 62 per cent of the non-unionized—scarcely a difference of great moment.[25] Equally, despite the greater strength of the CGT in our factories, the workers were less likely to endorse nationalization than was the case nationally, thereby suggesting that there is little relationship between the numerical strength of the CGT in a firm and its ability to mould the social attitudes of the workforce.

A more plausible explanation for the relatively low degree of influence of exposure to union ideology, we would suggest, is the low legitimacy that workers accord to the unions' efforts to exercise an influence on their views about society. The French unions were essentially attributing to themselves a political role—not so much in the sense of directly urging support for a particular party—but rather by attempting to influence workers' views about the inherently political question of the organization of social and economic power in society. However, it is clear that the majority of French workers rejected in a quite categoric way the right of unions to seek to influence their political beliefs. When asked: "Do you think that unions should seek to influence the views that people have about politics?", 84 per cent of French workers replied that they should not. This was not a peculiarity of our sample. A national survey of the French working class in 1969 put the question in even harsher form: 'Some people say "Workers should no longer follow the unions because they are too concerned with politics and not enough with defending the workers' interests at work".' Fully 54 per cent of the national sample agreed, while 36 per cent disagreed and 10 per cent had no opinion.[26] In this respect the French workers were very similar to the British workers we studied, of whom 93 per cent rejected the right of the unions to influence political opinion. Indeed we seem to be dealing here with a cultural norm of very considerable prevalence.[27]

The reasons for workers' antipathy to the wider social and political propaganda within the factory clearly needs much more careful and systematic study. However, one point that emerges from those comments that were noted down by the interviewers to this question is that part of the disapproval of the unions' ideological activity arose from the fact that politics was regarded as a highly divisive factor in the workforce, weakening its unity in their struggle with their employers. Attempts to bring the workers out on strike against government policies could only impose a major strain on the support of the significant minority of the work force whose political loyalties were firmly Gaullist. A related complaint was that the 'political' character of the unions resulted in there being several of them and this too was regarded as a source of weakness. Our case studies suggested that there was much truth in this. The ideological rivalry of the unions made the co-ordination of strike activity much more difficult, while fragmented strike activity opened the path for selective reprisal by management. We can get some idea of the problems of the desire for greater unity between the unions from a survey carried out by *Sondages* in 1969. People were asked: 'In your opinion, is it preferable that salaried workers in a country should be represented by a single union or by several?' 53 per cent of salaried workers would have preferred one single union, 40 per cent thought it preferable to have several, 7 per cent were of no opinion.[28] French workers appear then to have been dissatisfied with the highly divided system of unionism with which they were confronted and part of the blame for this was put down to the unions' emphasis on political objectives at the expense of the everyday struggle for economic advantage on the shop floor. It seems then possible that the reluctance to legitimise a political role to the unions in relationship to the workforce stems from an appreciation of the implications of political division for worker unity and for the capacity to effectively contest the immediate employer.

The evidence, then, in support of the thesis that the French unions are able to use a position as trusted opinion leaders to give or 'teach' workers a specific interpretation of their society seems rather weak. Members of the CGT were only marginally more radical than the non-unionized in the factories we were studying, and, from the limited data available, this would appear to be equally the case within the wider working class. Members of the other major union of mobilisation—the CFDT—were actually more moderate than non-unionized workers. French workers appear to have been markedly unreceptive to the unions' efforts at political indoctrination and rejected them as an illegitimate extension of the proper sphere of union activity.

THE INDIRECT EFFECTS OF THE PATTERN OF UNIONISM

It is important to remember that the French trade unions themselves would probably not have accepted the relatively simple thesis that trade unions exercise their influence by interpreting reality for their members in the sense of 'teaching' them the appropriate response to given forms of social change. Rather they stressed the importance of educating workers indirectly by making them aware of the exploitative character of capitalist relations of production in the course of their direct experiences in the factory. This has been accompanied by emphasis on the importance of involving workers in forms of action—whether petitions, demonstrations or strikes—which would make the conflictual character of management/worker relations more transparent. It is possible then that trade union influence is less a result of direct doctrinal persuasion than an indirect result of their efforts to sustain high levels of resentment against management and conflictual relations within the firm. In this way, workers' experience of conflict of interest at work will be more intense, the experience of work will be more salient in their lives, and their experience of social relations in the firm will have a more pervasive influence on their image of society.

Hamilton's surveys contained very little data on the pattern of social relations in the firm and this imposed important constraints on his analysis. He was perfectly aware of this and recommended that it should be the subject of further research. In a scathing critique of theories of embourgeoisement that emphasised the sphere of consumption to the neglect of the major differences that existed between working and middle-class work environments, he pointed to the prevalence in the former of 'authoritarian, hierarchical and punitive social relationships' and suggested that this was likely to be a persisting source of social grievance.[29]

We can only treat this question in a rather cursory way here, but the indications are that the character of social relationships in the firm provides a more powerful explanation of the class resentment of French workers than any direct exposure to union ideology. One factor that distinguished the French workers sharply from their British colleagues was that they were considerably more likely to see the firm in exploitative terms. In a question focusing on the image of management, workers were asked whether they thought that management was primarily concerned with the interests of workers, with the interests of shareholders or with the interest of everybody. Whereas, in Britain a majority of the workforce saw management in essentially 'co-operative' terms and believed that it was concerned with furthering the interests of all parties, in France an overwhelming majority thought that management was only concerned with the interests of the shareholders. 67 per cent of the French had this 'exploitative' image of management compared with only 34 per cent of the British.[30]

Of the variables available from our study, it was this perception of social relations in the firm that had the strongest effect on French workers' diffuse sense of grievance about class inequality in the wider society. In particular, the sense of class division at work was closely associated with French workers' belief that their class position had major implications for the overall quality of their lives.

68 per cent of French workers who had an exploitative image of the firm felt that workers had considerable disadvantages in their lives because they were workers, while this was the case with only 38 per cent of those who perceived relations as co-operative. The gamma correlation of association between the perception of the firm and the sense of wider class disadvantage is 0.509. Further, the influence of the perception of the firm is systematically more powerful than the influence of direct

exposure to union ideology as indicated by union membership for each of the main indicators of class radicalism that we have been considering. (Table 4).

TABLE 4

ATTITUDES TO INEQUALITY AMONG FRENCH WORKERS
BY UNION AND BY PERCEPTION OF MANAGEMENT

(Gamma)

	Union	Perception of Management
Disadvantages in life of being a worker	.17	.51
Differences in standard of living between businessmen and workers	.16	.52
Legitimacy of differences in the standard of living	.26	.41
Influence of Big Business over major political decisions	.10	.37
Fairness of taxation system	.28	.39
Class bias of taxation system	.14	.19
Methods of reducing inequality*	.10	.27

(* This measure was dichotomized into those favouring political means and those seeing inequality as inevitable or as dependant on economic growth)

However, it is clear that the unions played an important role in sustaining this antagonistic social climate within the French factories. They did this in two rather different ways. The first was an outcome of their purposive and sustained agitation against the policies of management and the second was an indirect consequence of their relationship to the institutional structure of the firm.

First, the French unions' principal agitational objective was to mobilise workers into direct confrontation with their own immediate employers. The development of highly automated forms of production does help to reduce some of the more traditional sources of working-class grievance: for instance it was easier for management to pay relatively high salaries and it takes away much of the physical arduousness and sheer monotony of work. It does then provide a favourable setting for an image of a progressive and socially-oriented management *in so far* as workers are comparing their situation with more traditional forms of work. Faced with this situation, the French unions set out actively to undermine the 'integrative' potential of the highly automated setting by stressing the new types of disadvantages that it threw up for the workers' lives: in particular they focused agitation on the dangers for health involved in the use of continuous shift work and the dangers for physical safety involved in prevailing manning policies. Further, they sought directly to counter the impact of higher salaries by laying great stress on the very substantial profits that the employers were making. In this way, they actively sought to sustain an image of the employer as exploiting the work force in a situation which at first sight might have appeared favourable to the development of more harmonious relations.

It seems clear that the unions did achieve some success in this direct effort to colour the image of management. Some 77 per cent of CGT members thought of management as exploitative compared to 53 per cent of the non-unionized. The unions were notably more successful in their polemic against the workers' immediate employers than they were in influencing wider social attitudes. The gamma association between union membership and the image of management is .360 compared to a maximum of .279 with any aspect of workers' attitudes to the wider society. Further, while the associations that did prevail with these more general attitudes towards inequality shrink heavily if one controls for workers' party preferences, the association with the image of management actually grows stronger (a partial gamma of 0.408). Finally, whereas previously there was a rather poor fit between the order of union radicalism and the radicalism of their respective memberships because of the rather anomalous attitudes of the CFDT members, this problem disappears when we consider union influence on the image of management. CFDT members are substantially more radical than either the non-unionized or members of the reformist union *Force Ouvrière*.

The second way in which the type of unionism in France may have influenced the way in which workers saw management was somewhat paradoxically through their very low degree of influence on the decision-making structure of the firm. The French unions would have been reluctant on ideological grounds to engage in any far-reaching process of institutionalisation of union-management relations, although they have frequently shown themselves prepared to engage in limited negotiations on issues affecting specific aspects of the workers conditions of employment or of the work situation. However, this ideological reluctance of the French unions to secure a higher degree of control over management decisions has undoubtedly been reinforced by the difficulty they face in doing so, due to the internal rivalry between unions and to the fragile relations with the base that flows from their intentionally politicised form of unionism.[31] The French unions have traditionally lacked the coercive power that has enabled British unions to make very substantial inroads on management prerogatives. At all events their influence on decision-making within the firm has been very slight indeed, and workers have been confronted with a form of management which is at best paternalistic and at worst thoroughly autocratic.

I have suggested elsewhere that the low participative character of the French institutional system leads to a very low level of legitimacy of the decision-making system and generates a high level of resentment against specific substantive decisions and dissatisfaction with the pattern of work organization. The combination of these effects provides a powerful inducement to conceive of relations between management and workers primarily in oppositional terms and is conducive to the development of an 'exploitative' image of the firm.[32] Some of the implications of the French institutional system become apparent if we consider the effect of the degree of dissatisfaction of workers with decision-making procedures for their image of management. Where French workers were satisfied with the institutional system, only 37 per cent viewed management as essentially exploitative; where on the other hand they were deeply dissatisfied with the institutional system, some 83 per cent saw management as exploitative (Table 5).[33] French workers' image of management was, then, closely related to their sense of powerlessness over the decisions that affected the quality of their lives at work. It was only where French workers had come to feel frustrated with the autocratic way in which management policies were drawn up and imposed that they were markedly more likely than British workers to have developed an image of their employer as exploitative.

TABLE 5

SATISFACTION WITH THE DECISION-MAKING PROCEDURES OF THE FIRM
AND THE PERCEPTION OF MANAGEMENT
(France)

Satisfaction with Decision-Making Procedures	Perception of Management as Exploitative
High	37% (N=14)
Medium	60% (N=93)
Low	83% (N=88)
(Gamma 0.43)	

UNION AND PARTY

Hamilton's thesis was that the French trade unions played a critical role in providing support for the French Left by sustaining workers' sense of social injustice in society. However, if the unions have little direct influence on workers conceptions of class inequality, then the theoretical connection between union membership and party becomes problematic. Yet there can be little doubt that the evidence suggesting an important association between party and union is both marked and consistent across time. For instance, if we accept Hamilton's Pro-Soviet indicator as reflecting attachment to the Left, 74 per cent of CGT members were pro-Soviet in contrast to only 28 per cent of the non-unionized, a difference of some 46 per cent. If we check the same relationship on rather better data in the 1960s, the general impression of the importance of the connection between union and party is confirmed. In 1967 82 per cent of male manual workers in the CGT supported the Left compared to only 44 per cent of those with no union affiliation.[34] Similarly, our own data would appear to confirm Hamilton's more specific argument that this relationship holds in the more affluent sector of the working class. Of the workers in our French sample, 71 per cent of CGT members favoured the Left, as against only 35 per cent of the non-unionized. But if the unions have only a small degree of direct influence on workers' attitudes to social inequality, how can we explain this persistent association between union membership and political preference?

A clear answer to this must await further research, but one plausible explanation might be that there is a process of self-selection; that workers choose whether or not to join the CGT in function of their pre-existing political attitudes. As we have seen, there is a substantial tension between the unions' objectives of social and political mobilisation and the prevalent norms in the French working class which reject attempts by the unions to influence workers political opinions. However, it would seem probable that this aspect of the unions' activities poses considerably greater difficulties for some workers than for others. For those workers who are anyhow inclined to support the Left, their belief that the unions are going beyond their proper function in their efforts at political mobilisation is not accompanied by any real degree of contradiction between the quasi-political actions that they find themselves involved in as union members and their underlying political loyalties. For supporters of the French Right, however, participation in strikes that are more or less explicitly directed against the government can involve a much more serious conflict of allegiance. While some right-wing workers will no doubt still join the CGT on the grounds that it provides the most efficient defence of their interests at work, we would expect that right-wing workers would be substantially less inclined than left-wing to join a union whose philosophy conflicts sharply with their own. The association between union membership and left-wing party support may then reflect little more than that right-wing workers tend not to join the CGT.

It is very difficult to establish the direction of causal influence in cases like this, but there are at least some indications that self-selection may have been at work. First, French workers tend to claim that they have always supported the same party. 74 per cent of workers in Hamilton's sample said that they had always voted for the same party; 79 per cent of male manual workers claimed to have always voted for the same party or tendency in the national election study of 1967, and the same was true of 82 per cent of our refinery workers in the early 1970s.[35] Now it might be argued that, even if we were to accept as accurate these remarkably high levels of reported party or spectrum loyalty, these workers may equally have spent most of their lives as members of the CGT. However, in the case of our refinery at Dunkirk at least we know that this is not the case. The workforce was recruited mainly in the late '40s and early '50s, but the CGT only gained a substantial following in the refinery towards the end of the 1950s. For most of these workers membership of the CGT would almost certainly have postdated their initial participation in the electorate.

A second indication that prior political beliefs may have affected choice of union emerges if we look at the political loyalties of the parents of unionized and non-unionized workers. Where left-wing workers come from families that were already left-wing, it seems probable that their attitudes may have been influenced well before they entered the workforce. If we compare CGT members with the non-unionized by the political loyalties of their families during their childhood there is in fact a marked difference in pattern. CGT members come more heavily from left-wing families than is the case with workers who remain non-unionized. In national samples about half of CGT workers come from left-wing families, while this is true of between 25 per cent to 30 per cent of the non-unionized. For our refinery workers, some 46 per cent of the

TABLE 6

FAMILY POLITICS DURING CHILDHOOD OF CGT AND
NON-UNIONIZED FRENCH WORKERS

Family Politics:	CGT	Non-Unionized
	%	%
Left	46	20
Centre and Right	17	29
No party/Don't know	37	51
	(N=162)	(N=45)

CGT came from left-wing families, compared with only 20 per cent of the non-unionized (Table 6). The percentages of workers who do not know their parents' politics are considerable, especially among the non-unionized, and it is difficult to know for these what subtler familial influences might have been at work. However the discrepancy in political backgrounds does suggest that part at least of the greater propensity of CGT members to vote left might well derive from patterns of attitude formed in childhood and have little to do with CGT membership as such.

Finally, if there *is* a process of self-selection at work whereby people choose whether or not to adhere to the CGT on the basis of their political views we would expect there to be a variation betwen workers who have some interest in politics and are therefore likely to be sensitive to the contradictions between union political objectives and their own political beliefs and those who are politically apathetic and for whom such congruence or lack of congruence will be a matter of relatively little psychological importance. The cell numbers for the politically interested right-wing workers oblige us to use a fairly crude form of classification, but the picture that emerges seems pretty clear (Table 7). Where right-wing workers have some interest in politics only about a quarter of them

TABLE 7

POLITICAL INTEREST AND PROPENSITY TO JOIN THE CGT,
BY PARTY PREFERENCE

	Party Preference			
	Supporters of parties of the Right		Supporters of parties of the Left	
Union Preference				
	Interested in politics	No interest in politics	Interested in politics	No interest in politics
	%	%	%	%
CGT	26	61	79	71
FO, CFDT	50	10	14	15
Non-Unionized	24	29	6	14
	(N=42)	(N=31)	(N=156)	(N=78)

join the CGT. On the other hand, a majority of the politically apathetic right-wing workers are willing to join the CGT. Interestingly, the pattern reverses itself for left-wing workers. Political interest among left-wing workers appears conducive to joining the CGT. This reversal of pattern is of course just what would be expected if self-selection is taking place. Among politically apathetic workers, the difference in the proportion of

Left and Right supporters joining the CGT falls to only 10 per cent, whereas among the politically interested it rises to 53 per cent.

The indications are then that there is a significant process of self-selection into the various French unions. Where workers come from left-wing families or are for other reasons committed to left-wing support, membership of an overtly left-wing union such as the CGT poses few problems. Where on the other hand workers come from right-wing family backgrounds or are politically aware right-wing supporters, then membership of the CGT would inevitably pose major problems of loyalty and hence there are powerful inducements to remain non-unionized or to join a union with less evident party preferences.

CONCLUSION

Does the presence of unions dedicated to fostering an image of society as one of class domination generate much higher levels of worker radicalism? On the whole, the evidence that we have been examining suggests that the *direct* impact of the unions' efforts to influence worker attitudes to society is fairly limited. While it is correct that French workers, in conditions of relative affluence and in a technologically advanced sector of industry, are considerably more radical than British workers in a similar setting, this greater radicalism characterises both the unionized and the non-unionized. Equally, there is a poor correspondence between the official objectives of the union organizations and the preferences of their respective memberships. It seems more probable that the sources of the social radicalism of French workers lie elsewhere.

In particular, we have suggested that the clash between workers' normative expectations and the paternalistic institutional structure of the French firm generates a series of tensions that lead to a much sharper sense of the inherently conflictual nature of relations between the workers and their immediate employers. It is this experience of social relationships in the factory that accounts best for the high salience of class inequality for French workers and it appears to provide an interpretative model that exercises a significant influence over their imagery of social relations in the wider society. The influence of the unions is thus real, but it is mainly indirect in type. They sharpen the sense of conflict over everyday issues in the factory, but more particularly they help to sustain the system of management that generates such a deep distrust of the French employers. They thereby play a key role in structuring the workers' experience in the factory and in fuelling the resentments that underly the French workers' interpretation of society as one of class exploitation.

NOTES

1. These differences have been elaborated in an earlier publication: D. Gallie, *In Search of the New Working Class,* Cambridge, 1978, chs. 10, 11.
2. R. Hamilton, *Affluence and the French Worker in the Fourth Republic,* Princeton, 1967.

3. See Hamilton, 278: 'The unions constitute the most important influence on working class politics to be discovered in this study'.

4. Hamilton offers an explanation of radicalism in small plants that hinges on traditions of rural radicalism.

5. Figures for French union membership should be treated with considerable caution. A calculation based on Hamilton's data gives a figure for the CGT of around 27 per cent. Adam *et al.*, *L'ouvrier français en 1970*, Paris, 1970 give 20 per cent for 1969. Unlike Hamilton, I have based the figures for 'sensed injustice' on the total sample. By cutting out non-response in surveys where non-response is high, Hamilton's method of presentation risks giving us a somewhat exaggerated view of the radicalism of the French working class.

6. For the greater capacity of larger plants to reward, see Hamilton, 222; for a clear statement of the general argument, 228.

7. The first two of these were carried out by the *Institut français d'opinion publique*, the third by the *Institut national d'études démographiques*.

8. Hamilton, 117.

9. For a more detailed discussion of the research design, see: Gallie, *In Search of the New Working Class*, ch. 2.

10. Comparable schemes are to be found in M. Mann, *Consciousness and Action among the Western Working Class*, London, 1973, p. 13 and in A. Giddens, *The Class Structure of the Advanced Societies*, London, 1973, p. 111. These, however, are more specifically concerned with 'class' consciousness and hence give a privileged place to the sense of class identity and of solidarity with other workers.

11. The question was: 'Do you think that a worker has disadvantages in his life because he is a worker?' The choice lay between: A lot of disadvantages, quite a few disadvantages, few disadvantages, and no disadvantages.

12. W. G. Runciman, *Relative Deprivation and Social Justice*, London, 1966; R. Scase, *Social Democracy in Capitalist Society*, London, 1977.

13. The questions were: 'Do you think of yourself as belonging to a social class?' and 'When you compare the standard of living of a worker with that of the owner of quite a large business or of a lawyer with a big clientèle, would you say that there is: a big difference in their standards of living, quite a big difference, a small difference, or no difference?' The ability of British workers to provide perfectly coherent images of the class structure has been frequently demonstrated since the pioneering work in this country by Goldthorpe *et al.*, *The Affluent Worker in the Class Structure*, Cambridge, 1969, ch. 5.

14. The options offered were: wealth, manual or non-manual work, education, manners, or the difference between employers and salaried employees. 50 per cent of the French gave wealth as their first choice, 57 per cent of the British.

15. The follow-up question was 'Do you think that this difference is: completely just, should be less great, should be much less great or that there should be no difference at all?'

16. See, for instance, Mann and Giddens *op. cit.*, and F. Parkin's discussion of the 'radical value system' in *Class Inequality and Political Order*, London, 1971, ch. 3.

17. The relevant indices were derived from the question: 'How much influence do you think that the people or groups in the following list have over major political decisions?' Besides big business and the unions, the list included the French President (the British Prime Minister), Parliament, and Public Opinion. The choice lay between: very great, quite great, fairly small or very small.

18. The question was: 'Do you think that the taxation system in France (Britain) is: just, not very just, rather unjust, very unjust. Those who answered that it was unjust were then asked why.

19. Goldthorpe *et al.*, *The Affluent Worker in the Class Structure*, p. 154.

20. The exact question was: 'What do you think is the best way of trying to reduce inequality in society? Which of these views is nearest to your own? 1. The only way to make a big reduction in inequality is to work within the present

system of government, but to try to get a government that is more favourable
to the workers. 2. Inequality will be reduced naturally as the country grows
richer. So the most important thing is to get the economy running well. 3. The
only way to make a big reduction in inequality is to change the present constitution. 4. I think that there is very little that one can do about inequality.
It will always be much the same.'

21. Adam et al., op. cit., 135, and for the breakdown by size of factory: 136.
22. See, for instance, the discussion in R. Dore, *British Factory Japanese Factory*
London, 1973.
23. Adam et al., 172.
24. Hamilton, 233.
25. The data for the French National Election Study, 1967, were made available
by the Inter-university Consortium for Political and Social Research. The data
were originally collected by Philip E. Converse and Roy Pierce. Neither the
original collectors of the data nor the Consortium bear any responsibility for
the analyses or interpretations presented here.
26. Adam et al., 157.
27. See, for instance, the cross-cultural data presented by W. H. Form in *Blue-
Collar Stratification*, Princeton, 1976, p. 161.
28. *Sondages*, 1970, I, 100.
29. Hamilton, 290.
30. For a more detailed discussion of this data, see Gallie, *op. cit.*, ch. 5.
31. *Ibid.*, pp. 281-292.
32. *Ibid.*, p. 206ff.
33. The index of satisfaction with decision-making procedures in the firm is based
on five questions asking people how decisions about shift work, manning,
salaries, company budgeting, and investment were in fact taken in the firm
and then how people felt they should ideally be taken. The level of dissatisfaction is simply the degree of discrepancy between the ideal and the perceived
methods. See for details, Gallie, *op. cit.*, pp. 131-134. The scores have been
grouped as follows: High (-15 to 0), Medium (1 to 10), Low (11 to 15).
34. Hamilton, 230; for the French national election data, see note 25.
35. Hamilton, 65.

European Trade Unions and the Economic Crisis:
Perceptions and Strategies

Andrew Martin* and George Ross†

In the years following the quadrupling of oil prices, the capitalist world has been in the most serious economic crisis since the interwar Great Depression. Trade unions, like most other economic actors, have consequently found themselves in a new situation, facing risks, and perhaps opportunities, different in important respects from those experienced during the preceding decades of relatively steady growth. How do the unions perceive this new situation? What is their understanding of the causes and character of the crisis? To what extent have they been led to modify their understanding of the economic and political environment in which they operate? What do they believe must be done to cope with the crisis consistently with their interests and goals? What strategies do they believe it necessary to pursue in the market and state arenas to get those things done?

To begin to answer these questions, we joined with some colleagues to study union leaders' perceptions of the crisis and its implications for their strategies in five West European countries: Britain, France, Italy, Sweden, and West Germany. This article is a preliminary report. We want to stress its highly tentative and incomplete character; we have concentrated on certain themes at the expense of others with which we are also concerned. The discussion is in two parts. The first presents country-by-country summaries of the principal union confederations' views of the country's economic problems, the desired solutions, and the strategies to bring them about. The second explores the patterns that can be discerned among these views and suggests some conclusions that might be drawn concerning union responses to the mid-1970s economic crisis. To make the most of the limited space available, we provide only a minimum of the general background that can be found elsewhere and none of the documentation to be provided later in the full report.

* Center for European Studies, Harvard University.
† Sociology Department, Brendeis University.

In the research project the work on Sweden and France, respectively, was done by the authors, while that on Britain was done by Stephen Bornstein and Peter Gourevitch, on Italy by Peter Lange and Maurizio Vanicelli, and on West Germany by Christopher Allen and Andrei Markovits. The authors gladly acknowledge their indebtedness to their colleagues in the project for material on their respective countries while completely absolving them of all responsibility for anything contained in this article. All, however, join in recording their gratitude to the Ford Foundation for its support of the project.

ITALY

There are three confederations, historically rooted in parties on opposite sides of the great divide in post-war Italian politics. CGIL, the largest, was closely tied primarily to the Communist Party (PCI), continuously in opposition although the second largest party. The smaller Socialist Party, a recurrent participant in Centre-Left governments, has also had a presence in CGIL. The second largest confederation, CSIL, was associated with the continuously ruling Christian Democrats. UIL, much smaller than either, was identified primarily with the minor Social Democratic and Republican parties, frequent participants in governing coalitions. However, these partisan identifications and ensuing divisions among the unions were substantially eroded. While the confederations have not re-established the unified organisation broken up in 1947, their important metal industry affiliates have partially merged, joint local and industry action is widespread elsewhere, and the confederations act together through federal arrangements set up in 1972. One product has been the evolution of an essentially common view of Italy's economic problems. The most important recent expression of that view is the statement issued at Eur in early 1978. Marking important modifications in a general analysis of Italy's economic problems and their solutions which the confederations first put forward during the recession at the beginning of the decade, and elaborated further during the much more serious recession precipitated by the mid-seventies international crisis, the 'Eur line' can best be discussed against the background of that analysis.

Its basic thrust is that Italy's post-war model of development is fundamentally flawed, putting the economy in a highly vulnerable international position, making it impossible to provide secure employment, deepening social and geographical divisions, and ultimately endangering democracy. These consequences can only be avoided by shifting to a new model of development. The central flaw is that the economy's growth has been tied to the export of low and medium technology consumer goods, whose competitiveness depended on wages kept low by migration from the south, rendering the economy increasingly vulnerable to growing competition from Third World producers. The regional imbalance thereby built into the growth model adds to its vulnerability by perpetuating agricultural underdevelopment and hence excessive dependence on food imports. The narrow industrial base also results in high import elasticity for both producer and consumer goods. This is aggravated by the neglect of housing and collective services, making private consumption an excessively large component of domestic demand while leaving vital needs unmet.

Instead of creating a more viable structure, the state reinforces the vulnerable one. The fiscal system, the large state enterprise sector, and public administration generally are deprived of their effectiveness as instruments for structural change in the interests of maintaining the clientilistic base of the governing elites' power. Their stake in preserving 'parasitic' sectors blocks the reforms necessary to turn the state into a means for structural change, while the industrial entrepreneurs linked to the political elites are thereby locked into a system preventing them from performing their functions effectively.

The unions see the impact of the mid-seventies international crisis on Italy's economy as a demonstration of its structural vulnerability, which the government's response did nothing to diminish. In response to the decline in foreign demand, increased cost of imported oil, and consequent deterioration of the balance of payments, the government relied on sharp restriction of domestic demand and devaluation. Thus, it sacrificed employment to the balance of payments while further diminishing the leverage of state investment as an instrument for structural change. It thereby created conditions under which the major industrialists sought to regain the power over wages and employment they lost since the 'Hot Autumn' of 1969, trying to improve the competitiveness of the existing export sectors in this way instead of investing in more internationally viable industry. Thus, the old development model has been perpetuated, so that any recovery is bound to be cut short by a new stop-go round. The consequences are continuing inflation, rising unemployment, increasing regional disparities, growing division of the labour force between those with regular jobs and those precariously employed or unemployed, serious shortages and deterioration of housing and collective services.

In the union view, the only way to break this vicious circle and provide a secure basis for employment is to put into operation a new model of development. Its central features are: reconversion of industry from the traditional export sectors to high technology industry enabling Italy to occupy a new place in the international division of labour; a reform of agriculture reducing dependence on food imports; a shift from private to collective consumption to further reduce the high import elasticity and make up the enormous deficits in education, health, housing and transportation. In effect, there must be a marshalling of resources now being wasted, transferring them from unproductive to productive uses, particularly for types of investment—in widening the industrial base, research and development, the South, collective goods—neglected by the present growth pattern. This cannot be achieved either by the state as it is or by the 'spontaneity of markets' whose restoration industrialists claim to want. Hence the state must be transformed into an effective means for implementing collective decisions about the pattern of growth. Essential to this are far-reaching reforms of the fiscal system, public administration and the state enterprise sector, as well as the state's capacity to influence investment in the private sector through incentives and micro-economic intervention rationally designed to achieve the necessary reconversion, planned in such a way as to assure employment while the process is going on.

What is urged, then, is not simply increased investment but investment directed toward transforming the whole pattern of growth, replacing the logic of private accumulation with that of social accumulation. While this is declared the only route to sustainable recovery from the present crisis, it is seen as well as the basis for a new kind of social development in which democratic values and social solidarity are more secure. Ultimately, the union view embodies a critique of capitalism and a vision of its replacement reflecting an essentially socialist perspective. Within CGIL and the PCI this perspective is largely shaped by the Gramscian version of Marxism, which focuses on the historically specific character of Italian capitalism, in its political and cultural as well as economic dimensions, rather than the general character or laws of capitalist development. This evidently fostered a highly concrete analysis of the economy which may well have been easier for CSIL to embrace when its disillusionment with Christian Democracy, following the meagre results of the 'opening to the Left', and the Hot Autumn combined to move it to the Left. Thus, the confederations could arrive at a common view of the economy at a time when events in both the labour market and political arena were pushing them toward political autonomy and trade union unity.

However, while a common analysis became possible, a common strategy remained difficult. The proposed shift toward a new model of development evidently requires a change in the state's role. The obvious way for the unions to bring this about would be to work for a change in the government's composition by supporting the party or parties committed or at least more likely to use the state in the prescribed way than the parties in power. But concretely this would mean supporting the PCI in its bid to end its exclusion from government. Doing so would abandon the non-partisanship on which such unity as the three confederations have achieved is contingent. As long as unity is regarded as worth preserving, even CGIL which goes as far as saying that democracy demands "the alternation of political forces in the leadership of the country" cannot risk supporting the PCI explicitly. Thus, it is extremely difficult for the unions to adopt a common strategy to establish the political framework within which the new model of development can be implemented.

In lieu of that, they have searched for alternatives. One was to try to influence the existing government by negotiating with it directly over national policy, backed by pressure in the form of general strikes and demonstrations—in effect, extending collective bargaining from the labour market to the political arena and substituting the union peak associations for political parties. The confederations pressed such a 'struggle for reforms' in pensions, housing, health, education, transportation and even the fiscal system beginning in 1969, shifting emphasis to employment and regional development—in fact, the new model of development—during the 1971 recession. While this strategy served to re-establish the confederations' role following the Hot Autumn, it had very little impact on social and economic policy.

Another alternative was to try to alter the pattern of investment by including individual investment decisions themselves in contracts negotiated with employers—in effect, relying on collective bargaining confined to the labour market but adding entirely new content to it. Beginning in the partial recovery from 1972 and 1974, major national unions, with the confederations' encouragement, demanded contributions to social services and commitments to invest in the South in negotiations for new contracts, succeeding in a number of cases. However, with the onset of the more severe recession in 1975, there was very little investment to bargain about. Although investment control through collective bargaining remains part of the unions' strategy, they were forcibly reminded that its effectiveness depends on economic policy beyond the reach of collective bargaining. The need to bring about the political conditions for a change in policy again proved to be inescapable.

In fact, the unions perceived the need as increasingly urgent, while the possibility of such a change seemed much enhanced after the 1976 election. The urgency lay in the consequences of continuing economic crisis. Increasing dispersion of growing unemployment was enlarging divisions and potential conflicts among different groups, ranging from those with jobs in relatively prosperous or protected sectors, through those in precarious 'black' jobs, to the growing numbers of 'marginal men', especially youth, with no jobs or any prospects of them. Particularistic action to protect living standards was increasingly likely by those in the strongest position, undermining the unions' cohesion and their ability to protect the weaker, and hence their claim to represent the whole working class, as well as their capacity to defend the gains in wages and workplace power won in the aftermath of the Hot Autumn. Not only were employers trying to exploit the situation to restore pre-1969 conditions but there was a real danger of a political crisis culminating in an authoritarian outcome that would destroy the unions along with the democratic constitution. The potential constituency for an anti-democratic mobilisation created by unemployment could be swelled by a disaffected middle class hurt by inflation, particularly in a tense atmosphere in which executive paralysis is also demonstrated by intensified terrorism. The economic crisis was thus seen as leading into a crisis of democracy.

The way out of the crisis urged by the PCI—the 'historic compromise' that would bring it into a new, broad coalition government—seemed to be brought nearer when support for the PCI drew even with the Christian Democrats in the 1976 election. However, the strength of the PCI's bid depended in part on the credibility of its claim that its participation would make possible an effective economic policy. This, in turn, was contingent on union acceptance of the PCI's view of what such a policy entailed. Both shared the general analysis pointing to the need for a new model of development. But the PCI increasingly stressed an additional element missing from the union view: the proposition that the unions' successful pursuit of escalating demands contributed to the crisis and that restraint and concessions by them were necessary to solve the crisis. It was this proposition the confederations accepted in the 1978 Eur line.

The earlier analysis provides its basic premise: the reconversion of industry and rise in collective consumption essential for sustainable growth requires an increase in investment and relative decline in private consumption. However, this cannot occur if wage increases channel all growth into private consumption. It is this implication for wages the unions failed to take into account in both their earlier analysis and labour market strategy. They treated wages as an "independent variable" that could be targeted to an increase in living standards to which the other economic variables would adapt. This was an illusion, for, in the CGIL Secretary's words, "in an open economy all variables are dependent on one another". The unions succeeded in protecting wages against Italy's high inflation, including the effects of devaluation, by winning their demands for indexation. But they must now moderate and stretch out wage demands in order to permit a transfer of resources to needed investment. Accordingly, they must negotiate revisions in the indexation formula to eliminate its tendency to increase wages more than inflation during a period of declining inflation rates. Overall, wage policy should aim primarily at maintaining real wages, concentrating increases beyond that on low paid workers. While acknowledging that wage developments may thus aggravate or alleviate the crisis, the confederations continue to insist that they are not its principal cause, as alleged by the government and *Confindustria,* the employers' confederation. Moreover, the unions regard wage moderation as contingent on participation in sectoral and enterprise planning, through representation, collective bargaining and rights to information, enabling unions to see that the resources thereby released are in fact used for the required investment.

A second major respect in which the confederations say they had failed to follow their analysis to its logical conclusions concerns the mobility of labour. The required shift of resources from unproductive to productive uses implies that some jobs will be eliminated. However, this was made very difficult by the unions' success in virtually eliminating management's right to fire. Now unions should negotiate to protect job security in ways permitting greater mobility, providing that unions retain control over it, by specifying the conditions under which there can be dismissals, prohibiting layoffs until alternative jobs are provided, and requiring special training and placement arrangements for the workers involved.

Supplementing these modifications in labour market strategy are others. Unions should regulate strike action in accordance with a strategy, including their wage and investment policies, curbing random strikes in pursuit of particularistic advantage or interrupting services needed by other workers, both of which fragment the working-class and enlarge the risks of counter-mobilisation and anti-strike legislation. While differences between the lowest paid and others should continue to be diminished, the egalitarianism originating in the Hot Autumn should be tempered to allow differences in pay for different types of work, as long as unions retain the control needed to prevent the restoration of occupational hierarchies and divisions in the working class.

Thus, the Eur line consists of modifications in union action described as essential to the general economic programme the unions themselves demand. It amounts to an offer of concessions in exchange for implementation of that programme. But since that programme is not likely to be implemented by the existing government, the offer is implicitly made to a potential alternative government, in which the PCI participates. The possibility of an effective economic policy if such a change in the government's composition takes place is thereby demonstrated, reinforcing the credibility of the PCI claim with respect to that possibility. Seen in this way, the Eur line represents a solution to the confederations' problem of designing a strategy by which they can contribute to the political conditions for realising their economic programme without compromising the political autonomy on which their unity rests. But doubt is cast on the viability of the solution in two ways: the widespread opposition with which the Eur line was met within the unions; and, more recently, the PCI's setback in the 1979 election, making the prospect for implementing the economic programme more remote again. Thus, the Italian unions' strategic dilemma persists.

FRANCE

The CGT, the larger of the two main confederations to which our discussion is confined, has been closely linked to the Communist Party throughout the post-war period. The CFDT originated in the Catholic confederation's secularisation in 1964. Marking a shift to the Left accelerated by May-June 1968, it declared itself socialist in 1970, though without forging formal links with the reconstructed Socialist Party. Thus, both view the French economy in the light of commitments to transforming it, but in accordance with contrasting visions of change. Nevertheless, from the beginning of the decade both shared a largely common analysis of the economy that underwent little modification in the context of the mid-seventies crisis, exhibiting the first signs of change only in 1978, following the break-up and electoral defeat of the Union of the Left.

The CGT's analysis has been cast in terms of the 'state monopoly capitalism' version of Marxism adopted by the PCF in the aftermath of the 1968 upheaval. From this standpoint, French capitalism had entered a new stage in the 1960s. It is distinguished by the subordination of the state to the fraction of the bourgeoisie controlling the monopoly sector in an effort to offset the declining rate of profit. To this end, the state's financial and administrative powers are turned to the restructuring of capital and intensification of rationalisation. Science and technology are thereby more completely harnessed to these purposes at the expense of human needs; the expansion of collective goods—education, health, housing, public transport, etc.—is stopped, and whole sectors are faced with extinction because they fall outside the monopoly sector, such as small-scale capital, or because of general transformations, such as those aimed at the rationalisation of distribution and finance. The basic contradiction between the socialisation of production and private appropriation is thus further developed.

The blatant subordination of the state to the monopoly caste's needs unmasks liberal democracy and hence the legitimacy of the very state on whose powers the monopoly fraction had come to depend more than ever. Failure to meet the needs of other segments of society generates a broad spectrum of opposition, not only workers but also *couches moyennes*—engineers, technicians, white collar employees, small-scale producers and retailers, intellectuals—even segments of the competitive fraction of the capitalist class. All come to realise, in varying degrees, the human potential inherent in advanced productive techniques which is blocked by monopoly control. Forming a potential majority, they provide the basis for a political transition from state monopoly capitalism to 'advanced democracy', which in turn makes a further transition to socialism possible. Such a transition offers the only remedy for the impact of state monopoly capitalism on these groups, but it can occur only if a coalition of all these groups is forged by the political Left. The strategic conclusion for trade unions is that their actions in the labour market must contribute to the mobilisation of that coalition.

This perspective dominated the ideological market place that CFDT entered as it moved leftwards in the 1960s and its analysis of the 'crisis of French capitalism' was broadly similar. CFDT distinguished its position from CGT's by condemning as economism the attribution of the crisis to the declining profit rate. To CFDT, it was a crisis of capitalist society in its entirety, due also to spiritual alienation in work and exploitation in the spheres of culture and consumption. Similarly, while sharing CGT's view that the only solution lay in basic social transformation, CFDT conceived of the transition to a 'new type of development' not as a political one but primarily a struggle to achieve *autogestion* by direct union action at the level of production.

The two confederations' common rejection of the existing mixed economy permitted no partial remedies within its limits, making it pointless to propose new techniques for managing capitalism however much they might go beyond the previous methods of demand management or indicative planning. Thus, their view of the French economy was entirely outside the universe of discourse in which mainstream economists and government officials debated economic policy. Since crisis was endemic to the whole development of capitalism, the more palpable symptoms of crisis in the mid-seventies—increased inflation, unemployment, regional and sectoral decline, attacks on social services—required no special explanation. What was simply revealed thereby was that state monopoly capitalism had reached the point where it could no longer counteract the declining profit rate, despite its control of the state.

The almost exclusively national focus of the analysis must be emphasised. If the international context in which French monopoly capital operated had become more difficult, the crisis remained a national one, for which there was a national remedy. This focus was reflected in the 1972 PC-PS Common Programme, which called for the nationalisation of many of France's large companies, particularly large transnational enterprise. It is even more marked in the CGT's own dis cussion, which almost entirely ignored the international dimensions of the crisis, suggesting an almost Gaullist confidence in the feasibility of dealing with its consequences by action in France alone.

The unions' principal response to the worsened economic situation concerned not its explanation but its implications for union action. To CGT, it meant that a cross-class anti-monopoly alliance and political victory of the Left had become all the more urgent and possible. Trade union action accordingly had to be geared to mobilising support for that victory more intensively than ever. CFDT, with its different conception of the function and hence forms of trade union action posed an obstacle to be overcome by a revival of 'unity-in-action'. Despite its alternative perspective, precluding explicit support of the Union of the Left, CFDT felt compelled to shift its view of what constituted appropriate union action. Rising unemployment was recognised as making more difficult the kind of militant, often prolonged, local strikes in support of 'qualitative' demands and ultimately *autogestion,* on which it had earlier relied. Now it agreed to the kind of action CGT regarded as necessary. The keystone of CGT tactics was the 'day of action', a symbolic strike lasting 24 hours or less and involving large numbers of workers. Accompanied by mass public demonstrations, protesting against the general symptoms of crisis —with slogans like "no to the dismantling of French industry"—and making broad demands such as for increased consumption, such activities were directed at national level bodies, such as industry associations, the CNPF, or the government itself.

This kind of action, intentionally for CGT and in spite of itself for CFDT, staked everything on the cohesiveness and electoral success of the Union of the Left. Only with its division and defeat in 1977 and 1978 did both confederations reappraise their long-standing perspectives on the economy. In CGT, these pointed in different directions.

The first rested on a critique of CGT's reliance on highly general, defensive action designed mainly for political mobilisation. This was condemned as inadequate because it tended to demobilise workers with respect to their own work situation, where their action would be essential regardless of the outcome of the election. Given the actual outcome, which removed the constraints on the government's economic policies imposed by the Left electoral threat, the strategy that had been pursued undermined the unions' capacity to provide a defence against the onslaught of austerity and rationalisation. Trade union action should have been based on a better understanding of the relation between crisis and politics. The crisis of advanced capitalism is more than an economic crisis: it is in fact a 'crisis of democracy'. It will be resolved either by a diminution of democracy or by its extension, particularly to the realm of work. Therefore, union action should combine resistance to attacks on democracy, aimed at enforcing the plans and policies required by capital, with struggle for alternative plans and policies, addressed to the problems faced by workers in specific firms and sectors as a result of the crisis. In mobilising workers to develop and push for such practical counter-proposals, the unions would become a 'proposition force'. But its function would not be to propose an alternative plan for managing the capitalist economy; it would be to develop workers' awareness of the possibility of alternatives, their capacity to develop the alternatives, and their consciousness that the implementation of the alternatives involves a basic social transformation. The very direction and substance of the transformation as well as the power to accomplish it would be the cumulative outgrowth of rank and file participation in the process of counter-proposition.

The unions' task would be to support the process by building up expertise on the structure and tendencies of the various parts of the French economy and their international positions and by organising the struggles for the counter-proposals. 'Proposition-force' unionism marked a clear departure from the conception of union roles that had prevailed in the CGT. It implied greater autonomy from the PCF and a more *autogestionnaire,* decentralising strategy and vision of change for the Left as a whole, opening up possibilities for renewed joint action with CFDT on different terms. In all of these respects, 'proposition force' unionism, already manifested in a CGT counter plan and joint action by the metal unions in the iron and steel industry, leading to negotiations, ultimately unsuccessful, with the government, has a clear and recognised affinity to the Italian unions' strategy with its focus on direct union involvement in microeconomic, sectoral problems.

The other position rejects this "Italianism" in favour of continued political mobilisation in support of the PCF's current view of the economic crisis and strategy for responding to it. With world imperialism in a profound crisis, France is being reduced to a completely subordinate position. Rather than resisting this, the French government pursues a 'strategy of decline' serving only to enable the monopolies—the French transnationals—to maintain their position in the restructured international economy at the expense of the rest of French society. While pointing to international factors more than before, the crisis in France is still described as 'above all national', due to deliberate policy choices. CGT's task is accordingly to co-operate with the PCF in struggling against all of the government's policies that sacrifice French workers and others to their strategy. This would mean not simply defensive unionism but political mobilisation aimed at restoring the PCF's position relative to the Socialists and a renewed effort to achieve political power and a national solution to economic crisis, implying a siege economy and possibly withdrawal from the Common Market.

In the CFDT, reassessment of its position began with the break-up of the Union of the Left. This led to no significant modification of its economic analysis except that it too gave greater attention to changes in the international division of labour, with the emphasis on the strategic implications. Rejecting autarchic solutions, the CFDT affirmed the need for extending trade union action on the European level, through the ETUC. Concerning France itself, the 'day of action' approach was rejected as sacrificing the articulation of rank and file responses to experienced conditions in the interest of misdirected political mobilisation. Instead, it was necessary to return to workplace and branch-level action in support of demands, not only for material improvements but also for increased worker power, leading toward a change in the model of development. It was re-emphasised that such action was the essential ingredient of the kind of change to which CFDT was committed and a precondition for any support of the process of change that could, or should, be organised in the political arena. For some, this marked a reassertion of the *autogestionnaire* conception of social transformation built up in the early 1970s. To others, it represented a shift toward collective bargaining limited to more conventional, bread-and-butter union goals, without the transformative implications of workers' control, responding to an allegedly increased willingness of the CNPF and government to enter into such limited contractualism.

In both CGT and CFDT, then, there are signs of change in contrasting directions. Whichever directions prove dominant, it is evident that they embody reappraisals of the strategic possibilities for unions in the light of the fundamental change in the political context of union action resulting from the Left's 1978 election defeat.

SWEDEN

There are two main confederations, the larger LO consisting of blue collar unions and TCO of white collar unions. From its establishment by the Social Democratic Party at the turn of the century, LO has been linked to the party which governed Sweden for nearly four and a half decades until 1976. TCO, growing rapidly in the post-war period, is formally non-partisan. In response to the belated impact of the mid-1970s international crisis the two confederations adopted positions that have much in common. These positions flow from an analysis of Sweden's long range economic problems that was already being developed, principally by LO, in the early '70s. This analysis departed from the position Swedish unions had held throughout most of the preceding post-war period. Shared in some important respects by Swedish capital, the earlier position entered into a consensus around the 'Swedish model'. An erosion of that consensus was already evident in the union analysis emerging in the early '70s but went much further as union and business interpretations of the crisis diverged more sharply.

As elaborated by LO, the thrust of the earlier position was that micro-economic decisions could be left to the capitalist firms that ran the bulk of Swedish industry, as long as the economic environment of the decisions was shaped by a specific combination of state and union policies. This policy mix was believed to make it possible for Sweden's small, open economy to satisfy the unions substantive goals of full employment and rising consumption (of collective as well as private goods) while preserving the organisational autonomy and cohesion on which the continued pursuit of the required policies was assumed contingent: above all, continued control of the state by the Social Democrats.

In this view, the state's main function is to carry out a version of

Keynesian policy going beyond simple demand management. One feature of this version is a calibration of general fiscal measures so as to stabilise the investment component of demand, shifting investment from booms to slumps through variations in company taxation. Another is the use of selective manpower policy measures on an exceptionally large scale. This is expected to permit the supply of labour to be acceptably adjusted to shifts in demand produced by continuing change in industrial structure, regarded as the key to maintaining the economy's international viability.

One major function of union wage policy is precisely to keep up the pressure for such structural change. Wage bargaining is co-ordinated by LO in order to enforce a 'solidaristic wage policy' of equal pay for equal work, regardless of a firm's profitability. This is assumed to force less profitable firms to become more efficient or shut down, while more profitable firms are enabled to finance their own expansion sufficiently to maintain the economy's international competitiveness and employ- ment. Co-ordination of wage bargaining on this basis is expected to limit particularistic action by individual unions. On the one hand, this is tacitly understood as essential to maintain the political cohesion among LO unions needed for them to be effective in mobilising electoral support for the Social Democrats. On the other, this is more explicitly described as avoiding inflationary inter-union wage rivalry. While this provides a partial equivalent to an incomes policy, any formal incomes policy in which the state is involved is ruled out in order to preserve the flexibility needed for a wage policy capable of retaining the unions' consent to co-ordinated bargaining. Since the requirements of consent are recog- nised as limiting the extent to which such bargaining can restrain the aggregate level of wage increases, the main burden of achieving non- inflationary full employment is left to the combination of demand management and structural change.

The exceptional extent of Swedish unions' earlier acceptance of struc- tural and technological change rested on their confidence that full employment would be maintained and that manpower policy effectively shifted the costs from the workers who had to change jobs to the society as a whole. However, doubts on both scores accumulated during the later 1960s. By the end of the decade, unions were becoming convinced that microeconomic decisions could not in fact be left to management, and that structural and technological change had to be subject to greater control by both the state and unions. This was translated into the Social Democratic government's policies in two ways. One was an industrial policy, including the creation of new instruments such as a state invest- ment bank, a holding company for state enterprise, and a ministry of in- dustry. The second was a cluster of legislation on industrial democracy, giving unions rights to get information on and bargain over any issue concerning enterprise planning and workplace organisation, increasing job security, and strengthening work health and safety requirements together with union power to enforce them.

While these initiatives expanded state and union control over the direction and location of new investment as well as the quality of work associated with it, they provided little leverage on the volume of investment. Yet, the amount of structural change and corresponding investment needed to maintain the Swedish economy's external equilibrium was perceived to be increasing during the 1970s. Along with virtually all other actors in the political economy, the unions accepted this view. However, they developed a conception of how to meet the need that diverged increasingly from a Swedish business solution. Starting at a macroeconomic level, the union analysis points out that an increase in the rate of investment pre-supposes a corresponding decline in the growth of consumption based overwhelmingly on wages. Given the scope and corresponding power of the unions, the shift from consumption to investment can only come about if the unions allow it. This the unions would be willing and able to do only if two requirements are met. One is that the shift does not lead to unacceptable distributive consequences. The other is that the increased savings made possible by the decline in workers' consumption growth is actually used for the necessary investment.

The first requirement arises because of the distributive effects built into increased investment by capitalist firms, the necessary increase in profits exacerbating the already highly concentrated wealth and power of their private shareholders, which is unacceptable. The unions do not see nationalisation as a live short-term option and are divided over its long-term desirability. They propose to get out of the dilemma by channelling an increase in savings through collective mechanisms, which are of two main types. One is essentially the tax mechanism, accumulating a surplus to build up central funds that would in turn finance investment directly by purchasing shares, or indirectly through a variety of public financial intermediaries or development agencies that might also buy shares or provide capital in other forms, as already done by the national pension funds introduced in 1960. The other type is essentially a mechanism for the partial collectivisation of business savings. A portion of business income not paid in wages—of profits—would be assigned to a system of so-called 'wage-earner funds', administered wholly or partly by unions. The savings accumulated in that form would be made available for investment in various ways, depending on how the funds are designed. As originally proposed by LO, the funds would get a portion of profits in the form of directed issues of new shares, providing the firms generating the profits with an increase in equity capital while the corresponding ownership rights—of control and income—would accrue to the funds. This would eventually give the funds controlling shares in the firms and ultimately convert the latter from privately to socially owned firms, a process LO sees as part of the transition to socialism. Rejecting this as a goal but accepting much of the underlying analysis, the TCO has been trying to work out alternative forms for giving unions control over a portion of the social surplus while avoiding or limiting the acquisition of ownership by the unions.

The two types of mechanism for collectivising the finance of investment are both conceived as contributing to the redistribution of control needed to meet the second prerequisite for an increased investment rate. However, considerably less than the whole social surplus is expected to flow through these mechanisms, and this would be insufficient for the needed structural change. Additional methods are therefore called for. The state's rudimentary industrial policy is to be expanded to approximate the scale planning is believed to have in France and Japan. But in contrast with both, there must be genuine participation by unions at all levels of planning, from formulation of national and sectoral programmes, through administration of the various capital allocation instruments, to enterprise and workplace decisions. Partly, the decline of production that can no longer be competitive has to be planned in order to minimise and spread the social costs and assure alternative employment in the affected localities. Mainly, planning is needed to enable the state to take the initiative in expanding internationally competitive production under acceptable conditions. This is to be done by channelling capital through its financial intermediaries in accordance with an overall industrial development strategy and stimulating innovation, not only by supporting research and development generally but also by 'organising demand', eliciting whole new, potentially exportable systems to meet needs defined by public policy, such as transportation, energy, pollution control, and renewable energy. While firms are still decentralised decision units in this conception of planning, it is viewed as a means for the state and unions to incorporate external or social returns into the definition of goals as well as decisions at all levels.

The main features of this approach had been set forth before the mid-1970s international crisis had its impact on Sweden, which was delayed and deflected into socially less visible forms. Still in office at the onset of the recession in most of the other countries, the Social Democrats tried to bridge the recession by expanding domestic demand and subsidising employment directly and through subsidies for production for stock pending the anticipated recovery. This expectation plus record high profits following moderate wage gains in 1974 enabled unions to win large compensatory increases for 1975-76. When the recession proved much longer and deeper, slowing the recovery of demand and the relative growth of labour costs in Sweden's trading partners, profits and investment plunged to the lowest post-war levels in 1977. Mass unemployment was avoided by massive subsidies to companies and expenditures on manpower policy, enlarged by the coalition of 'bourgeois' parties that replaced the Social Democrats in 1976.

When the crisis struck, the unions elaborated more fully the approach they had already developed. They counterposed it to the employers' analysis which blamed the economy's problems primarily on excessive labour costs and proposed to remedy not only by lower wage increases but also cutbacks in social charges, the benefits they financed, and the whole range of job security and union rights won in the preceding years. To the unions, this amounted to a futile as well as totally unacceptable effort to compete on the terms that multi-national enterprise and repressive regimes could impose on workers in the new industrial countries. By accepting much lower wage rises in 1978 and 1979, the unions implicitly conceded that a cost gap existed with some of Sweden's OECD competitors, allowing devaluations designed to reduce the gap to take effect by not compensating for the resulting price increases. Nevertheless, they held that this would still leave unsolved the basic structural problems, revealed by the crisis as even more serious than previously recognised. Moreover, they insisted that no solution to the problems was possible except one that not only preserved the gains won earlier but also met the further requirements they had specified.

As noted, however, the political division between LO and TCO prevents complete agreement over how those requirements should be met. It also precludes a common strategy to bring about implementation of the economic programme on which they substantially agree. While implementation is unlikely unless the Social Democrats return to office, only LO can explicitly devote its resources to making it happen. To avoid internal strains and defections to a small, conservative confederation of higher salaried employees, TCO must stay out of the crucial electoral arena.

LO's own strategic problems are further complicated by TCO's political stance. Even if the Social Democrats are returned, there is no immediate prospect for implementation of LO's wage earner fund proposal. In addition to being internally divided over it, the party is reluctant to go much beyond what TCO is willing to support, lest it jeopardise the electoral support it needs from at least some TCO members. For this reason, both LO and the party have long sought to blur the organisationally sustained distinction between blue and white collar workers, trying to foster a consciousness of common trade union and class interests that can expand the scope of the party's potential constituency, e.g. by legislation to improve pensions and union rights as well as by tailoring wage policy to draw private sector TCO unions into co-ordinated wage bargaining. By the same token, any moves by TCO toward positions identified as Social Democratic, particularly on non-wage issues, are seized upon by other parties' supporters, both in and out of TCO, as violations of its non-partisanship. This has been especially true concerning wage earner funds, which would encroach further on capitalist institutions than any reforms carried out by the Social Democrats. LO's version of the idea has elicited intense opposition by organised business, which has attacked it as leading to a 'trade union state' somehow equivalent to the East European regimes. This attack has been concentrated on TCO unions, leading them and the confederation to draw back from an endorsement of the idea they seemed on the verge of giving.

The Social Democrats have consequently hedged their commitment to LO's version, adopting it in principle but promising no more than to investigate its technical problems well into the 1980s. This puts LO in a classical dilemma. In the absence of measures to collectivise investment along the lines it regards as necessary for sufficient wage restraint to permit the investment required for a sustainable recovery, it cannot deliver such restraint without undermining its internal cohesion and the basis of the Social Democrats' political strength. But in the absence of such restraint, the economic policy of a new Social Democratic government may be impaired enough to make it lose the next election. The dilemma is intensified because all the unions are now under pressure to make substantial wage gains to offset real wage losses in the last two years. Under the circumstances, the unions are searching for some temporary expedients with which to reconcile their avowed function of protecting their members' real consumption with the increased investment they acknowledge to be necessary. In addition, they stress the need for at least some progress toward the control of investment that is the other prerequisite for restraint. While the potential for this was enlarged by the earlier 1970s legislation, its realisation now depends on collective bargaining, but what can be accomplished this way is still seen as contingent on whether there is a government that creates a favourable political context.

WEST GERMANY

The single confederation, the DGB, is formally non-partisan. Especially at the leadership level, however, it is closely associated with the Social Democratic Party, reflecting the deep historical links between its predecessor and the party. At its founding in 1949, the DGB adopted a programme of nationalisation, planning and co-determination which it hoped would securely subordinate German capital to democratic control and prevent anything like a recurrence of the Nazi era. In the face of Germany's reconstruction in the post-war international political context and the subsequent experience of rapid sustained growth, the programme was abandoned. In its place, the unions developed the confidence that a version of Keynesian policy combining demand management with selective manpower policy sufficed to manage that growth, providing there was Social Democratic participation in government to assure its implementation. Under these conditions, they believed that collective bargaining over wages and hours plus an extension of co-determination would assure the workers' share of growth. The mid-1970s international economic crisis evidently did not have enough impact on Germany to seriously weaken this confidence, although the unions perceived an increased danger of unemployment and were dissatisfied with the response to it by the Social Democratic-Free Democratic coalition government. However, their view of the required response involved little modification of the combination of state and union action on which they had relied in the preceding years.

The view of the political economy being evolved by the DGB during the 1950s was definitively formulated in its Dusseldorf programme of 1963. It prescribed what can be referred to as a 'Left' Keynesian policy in which the budget is conceived as the principal planning document, setting aggregate targets to be achieved primarily by general fiscal and monetary instruments, geared to an expansion of publicly supplied collective goods as well as cyclical stabilisation, and reinforced by policies aimed at curbing economic power and reducing inequality by promoting competition and extending co-determination. This prescription ran counter to the ideology, if not the practice, of the Christian Democrats 'social market economy', and the DGB anticipated that participation in government by 'their party' was a necessary condition for its implementation. The DGB's expectation was seen as confirmed after the Social Democrats entry into the Grand Coalition in 1966. Accepting responsibility for coping with the recession beginning in that year, the party made the adoption of Keynesian policy explicit in a 1967 Stabilisation Law. This also set the stage for the 'concerted action' meetings of government, business and labour representatives at which the unions agreed to an incomes policy providing for wage restraint during the forthcoming recovery. The unions also pressed for measures specifically aimed at helping unemployed workers to get new jobs, including expansion of retraining, placement services and financial assistance. Such 'active manpower policy' measures were incorporated in 1969 legislation by the Social Democratic-Free Democratic coalition that replaced the Grand Coalition.

It is essentially on this combination of demand management with wage restraint and manpower policy that the unions have continued to rely, with only minor modifications in response to successive disturbances. Thus, the wave of wildcat strikes in 1969 ended the formal agreement on incomes policy with the state and employers, although the unions responded in practice to subsequent government appeals for restraint. The unions also withdrew from concerted action when the employers challenged the constitutionality of legislation extending the form of co-determination in coal and steel to the rest of industry, although after much delay and less fully than the unions wanted. The most serious damage to the DGB's confidence in the basic formula for managing capitalism under conditions of Social Democratic government was done by the government's response to the effects of the mid-1970s crisis, but even this resulted in no major shifts in the union view.

Initially, the unions expected the post-oil crisis recession to be a brief conjunctural dip like that of the late 1960s. They began to realise it was more serious after GNP fell for the first time in the Federal Republic's history in 1975. What fully convinced them of its seriousness was the rise in 1977 of unemployment to more than a million, over five per cent, for the first time since 1955. They blamed this development on the government's failure to expand domestic demand sufficiently to offset the recession in the rest of the OECD area. This was not the whole problem, but it was the key to it.

According to the DGB analysis, a worsened international economic environment has increased the danger of unemployment, slowing growth and reducing the room for manoeuvre. The changing international structure of production has stiffened competition, especially in the old textile, shipbuilding and steel sectors, but also in the rest of industry. Adapta-

tion to this change has been made more difficult by the oil price rise
and subsequent recession in the OECD area. However, the unions have
little apparent doubt that German capital will continue the adaptation
on a scale maintaining the economy's still exceptionally favourable international position, nor do they seriously call into question the necessity
and desirability of the export-led growth pattern that adaptation serves.
What they have come to doubt is that the adaptation will take place in
acceptable ways, particularly as to its employment effects.

The danger they see is that unemployment will remain high or rise,
even if it falls for a time, precisely because of German capital's continuing success in achieving the rise in productivity needed to stay internationally competitive. That rise has been persistent throughout the
post-war period and may accelerate. In the past, two factors kept the
productivity increase from resulting in unemployment. One was the
parallel rise in demand, domestic as well as international, making it
possible to consume the growing output. The other is the concomitant
reduction in working hours, reducing labour input without a corresponding reduction in jobs. Both factors must continue if full employment is to be maintained, but they are not doing so sufficiently to avoid
all the employment consequences of growing productivity in the absence
of additional measures.

The DGB view is that demand has not been growing enough in recent
years because of the post-oil crisis international recession. Instead of
offsetting this by stimulating domestic demand, the German government
contributed to the recession at home by an excessively restrictive policy.
Even so, it was not until 1977 that union demands for more expansive
policies became urgent. Specifically, they called for the stimulation of
demand primarily through expenditure increases rather than tax cuts,
confining any tax cuts to individuals, so as to increase their consumption.
They rejected the business claim that less stimulus, operating mainly
through tax cuts on business income, would suffice to increase employment by stimulating investment. In the absence of sufficient domestic
demand, the only domestic investment likely is labour-saving rationalisation rather than employment-creating capacity expansion, with the rest
of any increased profits going either into private savings or foreign investment. On analogous grounds, the unions rejected the business
argument that wage restraint was now needed to increase profits and
therewith investment and employment. Instead, three things are needed.
One is state expenditures that expand public sector employment while
meeting real social needs and adding to the demand that elicits investment and employment in the private sector. The second is a less
restrictive monetary policy which permits expansive fiscal policy to have
its effect. The third is wage increases that keep up with productivity
growth, thereby maintaining labour's relative share of national income
and hence the demand required to consume the output made possible by
increasing productivity.

However, even if demand is increased as much as it can be without
threatening inflation—a concern which the unions share but which they

regard as over-emphasised at a time when inflation rates have fallen and unemployment has risen—it alone could not reduce unemployment as much as it must be. Two factors limit the effectiveness of demand stimulus by distributing its impact unevenly. One is the changing structure of industry. The declining sectors cited earlier create high unemployment in the regions where they are concentrated at the same time that labour shortages occur in regions with growing sectors. The other is rationalisation within the surviving and growing sectors. While eliminating some jobs, it reduces the skill requirements and quality of others. The first contributes to segmenting the labour market between workers for whom there is high demand and those in less demand because of where they live as well as their age, skills and sex. The second aggravates the process by reducing the demand for skills that various groups of workers have, shifting them from high to low demand segments. While expansion of aggregate demand can blunt these effects by creating new jobs, it cannot eliminate the effects. Since structural change and rationalisation are nevertheless accepted as necessary, other measures are deemed essential to avert their consequences.

First, the state has to carry out a 'structure policy'. This includes manpower policy measures, such as retraining and job transfer assistance, plus large investments in public infrastructure and subsidies to business in regions where the declining sectors are concentrated, and also the requirement that expanding companies locate new jobs in the declining regions and recruit new employees from among disadvantaged groups. Second, the unions should use their co-determination rights to see that companies comply with these measures and also use collective bargaining to impose further restrictions on how rationalisation is carried out, including requirements for alternative jobs at no reductions in pay and with the necessary retraining as well as regulations assuring sufficient breaks, safety, and other aspects of working conditions.

But even the combination of demand expansion with such policies to control structural change and rationalisation will not suffice. A third ingredient is needed and that is the reduction in hours. Pointing out that output doubled while hours worked fell by about a fifth over a 16-year period, the DGB concludes that there would have been mass unemployment if working hours had not been reduced from 48 to 40 hours during the 1960s. To avoid mass unemployment in the future, the reduction in hours has to continue, going down to 35 in the next phase. This is primarily a task for unions to carry out through collective bargaining, the first steps having been taken in the metalworkers' strike in 1978-79.

The unions' programme for coping with the effects of the 1970s crisis on Germany clearly does not embody any significant change. All of its main components—stimulation of consumption by expansionary budget and wage policies, adaptation to structural change through manpower policies and regional assistance, and the shortening of hours—were present in their position in the 1960s. At most, these components have been more fully elaborated and pressed more intensively.

Even so, the unions have found the Social Democratic-Free Democratic government insufficiently responsive. After macroeconomic policy was kept restrictive until 1978, it was finally given an expansive turn, but neither its magnitude nor its form complied with the union view. It provided instead for substantial tax breaks for business income, regarded by the DGB as incapable of achieving its purported aims, while failing to provide enough of the kind of stimulus that really mattered. Nor has the government heeded the unions' call for a redefinition of the central bank's statutory responsibility to include the avoidance of unemployment, as the government was required by the Stabilization Law of 1967. Government measures in the area of structure policy also ran counter to the unions position. A 1975 law cut back expenditures on some of the manpower policy innovations made in 1969 and changed the rules governing unemployment benefits in such a way as to force unemployed workers to take jobs that are worse than the ones they lost in terms of pay, qualifications, and location. These restrictions have recently been made more severe in administrative practice and pending legislation, while none of the requirements concerning hiring policy urged by the unions have been imposed on employers.

Disillusioned with their party, the unions appear to be giving greater emphasis to collective bargaining. To defend their members' purchasing power and blunt the effect of structural and technological change, they are evidently placing more reliance on whatever resources they can bring to bear in the market arena, including the strike weapon. This has made it necessary for them to search for new tactics to preserve its effectiveness in the face of heavy use of lockouts by employers, who are perceived as on the offensive against unions. Thus, the unions seem to be falling back onto traditional wage and working conditions goals most readily sought through collective bargaining. Yet, if the economic context in which the bargaining takes place is beyond reach through action in the state arena, the effectiveness of that bargaining for even those goals must be in doubt. However, the German unions see no political alternative to at least tacit support of the Social Democrats, for they are convinced they would be far more vulnerable to attacks on their very capacity to engage in any collective bargaining if the Opposition were in office. They do not seem to have any strategy for coping with this dilemma. On the other hand, its intensity is diminished by the still relatively favourable, and improving, condition of the German economy, in which the unions perceive no crisis, whatever the situation in the rest of the OECD countries.

BRITAIN

While there is a single confederation, the TUC, with long-standing links to a single party, the British Labour Party, there is within TUC and between the unions and party a varying diversity of views concerning

Britain's economic problems and what should be done about them. However, there was substantial consensus on these questions within the labour movement in the months prior to and during the life of the minority Labour government of 1974. In this period, TUC and the party worked out a joint programme referred to as the Social Contract. While some of the terms were subsequently fulfilled, those most central to the economic programme were not, confronting the unions once more with recurrent strategic dilemmas to which they responded in divergent ways.

The premise underlying the programme is widely shared among actors in and observers of the British economy. There has long been insufficient investment in industry, leaving an industrial sector too small to support the British economy in its changing international environment. And the diagnoses of this 'deindustrialisation' conflict. The unions (allegedly exacting excessive wages and disrupting production) and excessive growth of the public sector are most to blame, according to a view prevailing across a broad spectrum stretching across the Conservative Party, business, press, economists, and well into the Labour Party. The main alternative available to the unions was a diagnosis developed by the Labour Left, led by Tony Benn, and the TUC largely incorporated it in the understanding it reached with the party.

On this view, deindustrialisation stems from a persistent misallocation of capital and poor management of industry. Instead of being used for the modernisation and renewal needed to keep industry competitive, capital has been diverted to speculative investment at home or sent abroad in search of higher profits. Such misallocation results largely from control of the channels through which capital flows by institutions geared to the international monetary system and interested in rentier income rather than entrepreneurship—the City—and transnational enterprise intractable to conventional national policy—the "meso-economy". Much of industry is consequently obsolete, in its management techniques as well as technology. In the face of these financial blockages and entrepreneurial deficiencies, macroeconomic policy alone cannot overcome inflation and restore full employment on a sustainable basis. The reach of policy must be extended into the flow of capital, rechanneling it into the kind of investment needed for the regeneration of industry.

There are several interdependent lines along which this is to be brought about. A state holding company should be set up to perform the key missing functions, providing venture capital, through nationalisation, partial ownership, or loans, to existing or new companies with promising investment projects. The design of such projects would be a major function of planning agreements over investment strategy between state and management in large companies. A plan worked out at national government level would provide the framework for guiding the overall pattern of industrial development within which investment projects could be evaluated and the various forms of support coordinated. Unions would stimulate and oversee planning at the enterprise level, too long neglected by British management, through negotiation on planning agreements, participation in company boards, and other forms of industrial democracy down to the shop floor, buttressed by new rights to information and consultation in advance of decisions. Thus, creation of a new, more internationally competitive industrial structure would be accomplished by state and union intervention in the micro-economic decisions determining the composition of investment.

While macroeconomic policy alone could not suffice, on this view, it was assigned an important role alongside microeconomic intervention. Demand would have to be kept up for enough investment and employment. But demand should be stimulated through public expenditures rather than tax cuts because of the greater leverage the former gives on the composition of both investment, channelling it into essential social needs as well as industry, and consumption, targeting subsidies and benefits to the less well-off. It is also recognised that if demand is kept high enough to keep investment and employment up, the tendency for imports to exceed exports would continue until the "measures to promote changes in the structure of industry to improve its com-petitiveness" had a chance to take effect. Therefore, to avoid renewed balance of payments deficits that would force the government to restrict demand, temporary and selective import controls are necessary in the meantime. Otherwise, there would be insufficient investment and in-creased unemployment, jeopardising the whole restructuring process.

Substantial state intervention in the supply and allocation of capital, supported by sustained demand and import controls, and reinforced by union participation at all levels are, then, the main ingredients of the re-industrialisation programme. On the other hand, the adjustment of wage growth to the division between investment and consumption envisaged in the programme was given a subordinate role. An incomes policy administered by the state was ruled out. Once the preceding Conservative government's incomes policy expired, there was to be a return to free collective bargaining. However, a commitment by the unions to exercise voluntary restraint was understood to be part of the Social Contract. The TUC interpreted this to mean increases no higher than necessary to keep real wages from falling except for low paid workers. This was con-tingent not only on implementation of the re-industrialisation pro-gramme, including full employment, but also policies concerning in-dustrial relations and income distribution. The first embraced repeal of Conservative industrial relations legislation and enactment of new legislation on health and safety, employment security, trade union rights and industrial democracy. The second included a wealth tax, food and rent subsidies, pension increases, price controls and other measures to protect low income families. However, the restraint that this would make possible, in exchange, was not assumed to be necessarily enough to keep wage growth consistent with the rest of the programme. Thus, it was left to import controls to block the accommodation of any nominal wage increases that would otherwise threaten the programme by creating balance of payments deficits if they were translated into real wage increase through increased imports. The crucial role thereby conferred on import controls, opposition to entry into the EEC, and strong criticism of repeated sacrifices of growth and investment in the interest of protecting the pound, all reflect the view that the costs of Britain's integration into the international economy outweigh its benefits, at least in the form inherited from the past, and that adaptation to more viable forms of integration requires at least temporary insulation. These issues became more salient after Labour's return to office with a bare majority in the second 1974 election.

Reviewing the period prior to that election, the TUC found that the government had demonstrated its commitment to the Social Contract. Legislation carrying out many, if not all, of its industrial relations and income distribution terms had been enacted or was in preparation, macroeconomic policy was expansive, and implementation of the re-industrialisation programme was being mapped out. After the election, however, the temporarily strengthened Labour government responded to a sharp deterioration of the economy's external position by abandoning much of the programme that remained to be fulfilled. Inflation had been accelerated by the oil price rise on top of the preceding boom, triggering wage increases according to the threshold provisions in the final phase of the former Conservative government's incomes policy. When free collective bargaining was resumed upon expiration of the policy, wages kept going up, overtaking prices. This spiral, coupled with declining external demand, due to the deflationary responses of most OECD governments to the quadrupling of oil prices, precipitated a massive balance of payments deficit. Once again, the government responded by restricting demand and intensifying pressure for wage restraint, including the threat of a new statutory incomes policy.

In the face of this situation, the TUC felt compelled to go beyond the unions' vague commitment to restraint and to resume responsibility for a voluntary but explicit incomes policy in 1975, initially in the form of a flat £6 increase. At the same time, it insisted that implementation of the rest of the social contract remained an essential counterpart to its acceptance of more effective wage restraint. However, the government moved successively further from the agreed pattern of policy. It severely cut demand in a series of budgets, concentrating on reductions in public spending and allowing unemployment to reach the highest post-war levels, actually reversing wage trends before the restoration of incomes policy. In addition, it largely abandoned the programme of state- and union-led industrial restructuring. Removing Benn from its direction; establishing a state holding company with far less scope, funding and power; allowing planning agreements to become a dead letter; omitting other measures, and rejecting any restriction on imports, the government fell back on an industrial strategy that depended primarily on private investment under prevailing international trade and monetary conditions, as in the past.

The TUC contested the government's claim that its policies were the only way to avoid a run on sterling that would force resort to the IMF, even deeper cuts, and the risk of its fall from office. On the other hand, the TUC believed an open breach with the government could bring its fall, given its increasingly precarious parliamentary position. Thus, the unions were faced again with their classic strategic dilemma: a Labour government was pursuing unsatisfactory policies, but a Conservative government would probably do worse. Even so, a point may be reached where that risk can no longer enable a Labour government to gain union acquiescence to policies they oppose. That point had been reached in 1969 with Labour's introduction of anti-strike legislation, on top of several years of unacceptable economic policies. The readiness for militant resistance displayed by the unions then forced the government to retreat, although relations between them were not repaired sufficiently to get the full union support needed to avert defeat in the 1970 election. The succeeding Conservative government went ahead with the even more objectionable Industrial Relations Act against which the TUC mobilised non-compliance and which Labour then repealed according to the agreement through which the unions and party re-established their co-operation. Although the party was now failing to live up to other terms of the agreement, this did not bring the unions to the point of rupture with it again. The TUC continued to press for its alternative economic strategy, but in view of its desire to maintain a Labour government in office, it sought and got its affiliates' consent to another year of restraint under its supervision in 1976. When, in spite of everything, the government nevertheless felt compelled to borrow from the IMF on terms the TUC begged it to reject in 1977, the TUC still did not break with the government. However, it refused to administer any further extension of incomes policy in 1978, agreeing only that at least a year should elapse between wage negotiations.

By this time, inflation was considerably lower, a recovery encouraged by a more expansive budget seemed under way, and tolerance for wage restraint within the unions was wearing thin. In the TUC's judgment, the time had come for a new election in which Labour had a chance to restore its majority. This would provide the political basis for a new start on the re-industrialisation programme abandoned during the sterling crisis. To the TUC, this still was the only acceptable way out of Britain's deep and long-standing structural problems, and a Labour government the only conceivable political instrument through which it could be carried out. If the prospects could hardly be bright in view of Labour's past performance, with the possible exception of the immediate post-war years, it seemed the only available option. So, once again, the TUC and various union leaders pinned their hopes on Labour's re-election, and sought to avert or contain manifestations of rising discontent that might jeopardise that outcome. But the possibilities for doing so ran out, and having gambled on postponing the election for as long as possible, Labour lost.

By the winter of 1978-79, what was left of the consensus around the Social Contract had broken down within the TUC as it had between it and the party. Various unions voiced views ranging from straight business unionism to virtual withdrawal from the international economy and establishment of an autarchic siege economy. Moreover, a wave of strikes by individual unions and groups of workers in defiance of their unions erupted, bringing settlements far in excess of what the government declared acceptable, disrupting public services and food supplies, and discrediting the claim that Labour governments could assure union co-operation. This situation lent itself readily to a Conservative election campaign in which the unions and their internal organisation were once more pictured as the root of Britain's problems. The incoming Conservative government was committed to tackling these fundamental problems and to a much more radical diminution of the state's role in managing the economy than any of its predecessors had attempted.

Having acquiesced in the Labour government's retreat from their joint economic programme for the sake of keeping that government in office, the unions were now deprived of even that minimal advantage in the state arena. Once more, they were thrown back upon their resources in the market arena, under economic conditions that promised to be highly unfavourable for the foreseeable future.

A GENERAL COMPARISON

Thus far, the mid-1970s crisis has not by itself precipitated much change in the unions' conceptions of the political economies in which they operate. The impact of the crisis is typically assimilated within perspectives growing out of each labour movement's specific national experience, strongly conditioned by the organisational and ideological legacies of their histories, and evolving in response to changes that were already undermining the assumptions prevailing during the earlier postwar period. If anything, the crisis appears to have reinforced trends in union ideas that were already under way. Beyond that, the modifications discernible in union positions since the onset of the crisis seem to have been primarily in response to political developments that have affected the unions' strategic options.

The most decisive legacies shaping union perspectives on the political economy are those left by the formative events of the two world wars and subsequent political reconstructions. The unions' evolution has been especially conditioned by their relation to the bifurcation of the Left crystallised by the Russian Revolution and reinforced by the international political alignment established after the Second World War. The patterns set then divided the five national labour movements into two groups, depending on whether the dominant party of the Left was communist or social democratic—the French and Italian cases comprising the first group and the British, Swedish and West German the second. The main confederations in the two groups interpreted the different structures of constraints and opportunities facing them within contrasting ideological perspectives, including alternative frameworks for analysing the economy: Marxian in the first and Keynesian in the second case.

This division has been persistent enough to serve as an initial framework for distinguishing the unions' contemporary positions: in some respects they are roughly what we should expect them to be on the basis of the categories into which they fell in the earlier post-war period. However, there are other respects in which they are not. Thus, when we compare their analyses of economic problems and proposed solutions, we find similarities and differences among the national labour movements that cut across the earlier post-war division. On the other hand, insofar as we can compare their strategies—their views of action to be pursued in the market and state arenas—yet other patterns emerge.

When we compare economic programmes, one of the most striking developments is the extent to which the Italian and Swedish labour movements have converged toward a common position. This is especially true of the principal confederations in each country, but the other confederations share the position to a large extent. The single British confederation also came close to that position, but only temporarily. A brief recapitulation of the common elements in the three labour movement economic programmes may help distinguish this position from those of the French and German labour movements, which differ from it in sharply contrasting ways.

Industrial structures making each country's international economic position more vulnerable are blamed for increasing the danger of unemployment, susceptibility to inflation, and sacrifice of social needs. To bring about the changes required in those structures in ways consistent with union interests and goals, the microeconomic decisions shaping industrial structure must be subjected to state and union control. The state cannot be limited to macroeconomic intervention, for demand management, alone or with selective manpower policy, leaves investment to precisely the capitalist firms whose decisions, based on private rather than social returns, resulted in the present structures. Such decisions cannot bring about the required structural change except under conditions, including unemployment and inequality, that are unacceptable. The state therefore has to take over the functions of mobilising and channelling capital to assure sufficient investment of the right kind, identified by planning at the national, sectoral and enterprise levels, through instruments such as state enterprise and financial intermediaries, and various incentives and controls. Similarly, the unions cannot confine themselves to traditional wage and working conditions issues, nor can they agree to wage restraint without the power to assure that the released resources are used for needed investment. Unions must accordingly participate in planning at all levels, in a variety of ways including representation but primarily through collective bargaining. Thus, macroeconomic policy and wage restraint are necessary ingredients in the restructuring of industry but can perform their functions only in combination with intervention by the state and unions in the microeconomic decisions on which jobs depend.

Such an extension of state and union power to investment is conceived (as much by business opponents as union advocates) as introducing a fundamental change in the predominantly capitalist mixed economy.

Without involving much new nationalisation (none in Italy where the demand is for reform rather than expansion of the already large state sector), increasing state and union control over the appropriation and allocation of the social surplus is, in effect, expected to supplant the logic of capitalist accumulation by democratic choice of the composition of economic activity, what the Italians term 'a new model of development' or the Swedes call 'economic democracy'. The economy would remain 'mixed' in that private firms would continue to exist, but it would no longer be one in which the state merely seeks to shape the macro-economic environment in which firms, public as well as private, operate according to traditional capitalist decision rules. While still autonomous, decisions at the level of the firm would be geared to politically chosen development paths. Thus, the change would be toward some form of 'market socialism', in which democratic control is exercised at the enterprise and workplace levels as well as through democratic politics at the societal level.

The central thrust of this position, then, is that the problems generated by the existing mixed economy can only be solved by transforming it on terms acceptable to the unions. But this is not conceived as taking place through a direct assault on the property institutions on which capitalist organisation of the economy is based. Instead, the transformation is envisioned through a process that can perhaps be characterised as functional socialisation, leaving largely intact whatever private ownership there is but emptying it of its role in the firm's central function of investment decision-making. This vision of an alternative economy seems to transcend the ideological dichotomy between reform and revolution that was one of the main historical legacies of the Left. In their perspectives on change, LO and TUC, on the one hand, and CGIL, on the other, clearly belonged on opposite sides of the dichotomy in the earlier post-war periods. The process of transformation implied by the common elements in their economic programmes accordingly suggests that they have undergone a significant ideological evolution since then.

There is little evidence of such evolution in Germany and not much more in France, except for the development embodied in the CFDT. Moreover, in neither Germany nor France do the union economic analyses point to a failure of capital to adapt the structure of industry to changes in the international economy as the primary source of economic problems. On the contrary, industrial structure is seen as being adapted thoroughly, even ruthlessly, to the requirements of international competition. It is primarily this that generates the problems. However, sharply contrasting remedies are proposed.

According to the German labour movement programme, structural change is not necessary. Since capital has made it happen on a sufficient scale, there is no need for anything like the socialisation of the investment function along lines pressed in Italy and Sweden, let alone outright nationalisation. The problem is that the employment effects of the structural change have not been offset by sufficiently rapid growth of domestic demand. If the state pursues sufficiently expansive general fiscal and monetary policy, supplemented by selective measures confined largely to workers, and unions succeed in keeping hourly wages up with productivity growth, the required growth of demand can be assured. Thus, the programme continues to reflect the 'reformist' orientation, shared with the Social Democrats, that no change in the existing mixed economy is required to solve the problems arising within it consistently with union goals.

According to the French labour movement programme, on the other hand, the structure of French industry has been distorted by monopoly capital, sacrificing the needs of French society to the interests of the large, internationally integrated firms. Their power over the economy cannot be constrained by partial solutions, even those designed to socialise the investment function, let alone the mere management of demand combined with collective bargaining. Nothing short of complete socialisation, transferring at least the large firms dominating the economy from private to social ownership, can suffice to re-orient production to national needs. Thus, the programme continued to reflect the 'revolutionary' conviction, shared with the PCF and Left socialists, that the problems generated by the existing mixed economy cannot be solved consistently with union goals without transforming it in such a way as to lay the basis for a socialist economy.

In the process of trying to characterise the unions' economic programmes in such a way as to bring out their central tendencies, we have obviously simplified matters, obscuring differences both among and within the Italian, Swedish and British labour movement programmes, as well as points of similarity between some of them and aspects of either French or German programmes. More importantly, we have compared these programmes in isolation from the strategic contexts in which they are actually conceived. This can be misleading, for the programmes obviously do not necessarily tell us the goals that unions expect or hope to accomplish by the strategies they pursue. In some cases, the programmes may really describe the top priorities to which all action is geared, but in others they may be mere window dressing. They may also serve as bargaining gambits with governments, parties or other unions, or as symbols around which to sustain internal cohesion, or several of these or other functions simultaneously. Thus, important issues of interpretation have to be resolved in order to understand how the economic programmes fit into strategic perspectives. While we cannot attempt to resolve them here, we can point to some of the ways they arise.

All the programmes assign important if varied roles to the state, and unions in all five countries seem concerned to bring about the political conditions under which the state is most likely to perform those roles, especially by getting parties associated with the unions in one way or another into office. But a closer look suggests that unions may be as much or more concerned with other goals they believe are at stake in the state or market arenas. The British case brings this out particularly well.

In Britain, implementation of the TUC's economic programme was clearly predicated on a return to office of the Labour Party, which had indeed entered into an explicit agreement with the TUC to implement its programme. Just as clearly, however, none of this sufficed to secure implementation. Yet the TUC continued to support the Labour government, exerting its influence with remarkable success to sustain union compliance with the government's incomes policy, despite its failure to carry out most of the economic programme which had been understood as the *quid pro quo* for union co-operation. Does this mean that the TUC was not really concerned about what happened to its economic programme? If not, what was it up to when it got the party's agreement over the programme?

The Social Contract was evidently designed to repair relations between the unions and party that had been strained nearly to breaking point during the 1960s Labour Government. The divisive issue was the serious threat to trade union rights the unions saw in the government's legislative proposals, withdrawn in the face of strenuous union resistance. Its Conservative successor actually enacted what the unions viewed as worse and fervently wanted repealed. But this required not only that the Conservatives be replaced by Labour but also that Labour would in fact restore trade union rights, which could not be counted on after the 1960s experience. So the unions made a commitment by the party to do so a condition for giving it the support it needed to win the elections. This commitment was also part of the Social Contract and, unlike the economic programme contained in it, it was fulfilled when the Labour Party did return to office. Inclusion of the economic programme can be understood as contributing to the Social Contract's success by drawing into the bargain groups within the unions and party, particularly on the Left, that placed as high or higher priority on the kind of economic policy the party should carry out. A Labour government was not viewed as a condition for implementing the economic programme; instead, the economic programme was viewed as a pre-condition for a Labour government and, ultimately, achievement of the primary union goal.

If this interpretation is correct, it suggests that the British labour movement regards action in the market arena as the most important means of advancing their members interests. Moreover, given its highly fragmented and decentralised structure, such interests are presumably conceived in particularistic rather than class terms. The only objective common to all the unions, then, is the preservation of their individual capacity for defensive or offensive action, as the case may be, on behalf of their own members, rather than the management of the economy, not to speak of its transformation, so as to benefit the class as a whole, as implied in the TUC economic programme.

But it is not necessarily true that the TUC, as well as some individual unions, are not actually concerned with the economic programme. It might express what they genuinely believe necessary and desirable, while they see a Labour government as the only possibility for making it happen. However, they may really have no strategy for turning that possibility into a reality. Given the unions' organisational weakness and the magnitude of both the task prescribed in the economic programme and what it would take to get a Labour government to act on it, there may be no available strategy for doing so. At the same time, they have good reason to believe that a Conservative alternative would threaten even their very capacity to function as unions, while at least the minimum objective of preserving this capacity can be secured under a Labour government. This, in effect, leaves them in a position of hostages to Labour, which is thereby given a great deal of leeway to follow an economic policy opposed by the unions.

To what extent do the other labour movements' strategies leave them in a similar position? The German unions seem to fall into it to some extent. Without the formal links to a party like those of British unions (though not the TUC itself), they nevertheless seem to regard Social Democratic participation in government as no less a condition for implementation of their economic programme. But what they have to gain for their members from its implementation may not be as great in view of the German economy's vastly greater capacity for growth. This puts the German unions in a position where they can rely primarily on market action, which is what they seem to do, providing that their institutional capacity to pursue it is protected. Thus, what they now have to lose in terms of trade union rights in the event of a Christian Democratic government may well be greater, given the continuing strength and apparent legitimacy of repressive traditions in Germany. In other words, German unions may fall hostage to the Social Democrats in the same way as British unions do to the Labour Party, but the costs may not be as high while the risks attached to the failure of any conceivable strategy for breaking free may be considerably greater.

In the Swedish case, the question is posed differently since only LO is linked to the Social Democratic Party and explicitly contends that the party's return to office is necessary for implementation of its economic programme, although the non-partisan TCO largely shares this view. For LO, the policies pursued by the Social Democrats during their exceptionally prolonged control of the state, which were not only consistent with LO's declared priorities most of the time but often incorporated specific LO proposals, amply justifies its heavy reliance on this political alternative to the strike weapon which Swedish unions had relied on as heavily prior to the Social Democratic era. In exchange for the policy implementation, LO has much to offer the party in terms of political resources it needs. Union structure, coverage, and growing centralisation created the potential for political cohesion and mobilisation that LO has tried to realise, quite successfully, by framing both legislative and labour market demands on a broad trade union or class-wide basis. The Social Democrats depend on LO to perform this function all the more because it cannot expect open support from TCO, but can expect to gain some electoral benefits from positions LO succeeds in identifying with trade union interests shared by TCO. Thus, the party would seem to have a lot to lose if it undermines LO's capacity for mobilisation by pursuing policies running counter to LO positions. At the same time, the unions' organisational strength in the market arena, together with the improbability of any significant encroachment on trade union rights by non-Social Democratic governments, would seem to make the risks likely to face Swedish unions in the event of Social Democratic defeat a good deal less than those anticipated by British and German unions in analogous situations. This might explain why LO has not fallen hostage to the party so far, at least as far as its declared goals are concerned.

While this may have been true in the earlier context of steady growth, however, it may no longer hold now that the structural underpinnings of growth have deteriorated. LO is evidently convinced that the gradual collectivisation of profits it proposes is essential to preserve co-ordinated bargaining, and the political function thereby served, at a time when increased investment is needed to restore the structural basis of growth. But if LO fails in its effort to define its proposal as a common trade union position that TCO can accept, its ability to overcome the considerable resistance to its approach within the party would undoubtedly be impaired. The party might prefer to risk declining cohesion among LO unions, with no alternative politically, to the loss of support in TCO. Thus, the political division in the labour movement would no longer bolster LO's leverage in the party. At the same time, the bourgeois parties' clear shift toward a more market-oriented response to the structural crisis, enforced by weakening unions' market power through higher unemployment, increases the risks attached to a new Social Democratic defeat. Under these circumstances, LO's bargaining position relative to the party might be sufficiently weakened to force it to retreat on an element of its programme to which it appears strongly committed. LO may then be confronted with strategic dilemmas that look more like those that have long faced the TUC.

In both France and Italy, the strategic problems posed by plural unionism have been more pronounced than in Sweden, while in neither has the risk of falling hostage to governments in which associated parties participate been put to a recent test. However, the labour movements in the two countries have differed substantially in their strategic perspectives, particularly with respect to the relative weight they have placed on getting associated parties into office and action to be taken on their own towards goals transcending the limits of wages and working conditions. The CGT and CFDT both pursued market action to defend the immediate interests of their members, while also trying to link those interests with the need for a socialist transformation (a remote and abstract goal) differently conceived by the two confederations. With the rapidly improving prospects of an electoral victory by the Left parties in the mid-1970s, the whole weight of union action was thrown into the effort to mobilise support for such a victory. This was done at the expense of market action to defend immediate interests and even the organisational capacity to do so. Everything was staked on creating the political conditions for implementing a radical economic programme until the rupture of the Union of the Left. The Common Programme, to which CGT had been explicitly and CFDT tacitly and reluctantly committed, was evidently designed primarily to forge a Left coalition. When the effort collapsed as a result of the basic conflict between the Communists and Socialists, the unions were left in a poor position to pursue alternative strategies in the market arena following the inevitable victory of the Right.

In a special sense, then, the unions had fallen hostage to parties not yet in power. What if the Left had won? Simple projections of alternative scenarios are impossible, for the relationships and tensions among the different parties and confederations would have had to be very complex. As it is, divergent lessons are being drawn within the unions. If the 'proposition force' approach that has emerged within the CGT survives and grows, it promises important changes in the relationship between that confederation and the PCF, and consequently with the CFDT, including greater reliance on the unions' own resources to protect workers' interests by market action aimed at partial solutions going beyond the mere defense of wages and working conditions. With respect to both programme and strategy, French unions would then be moving toward an approach developed by Italian unions much earlier.

The struggle for reforms which the Italian confederations undertook jointly in 1969 marked the beginning of that development. It was their response to a number of factors that combined to define their strategic problems at the time, including their growing autonomy from the parties to which they had been linked, the absence of any prospects for a change in the composition of government that would itself yield changes in economic and social policy, and the need to redefine the confederations' functions after the decentralisation through which the militancy that exploded during the Hot Autumn was absorbed by the unions. The development continued in the early 1970s when the scope of collective bargaining by individual unions was also expanded beyond traditional wage and hours concerns to the level and location of the investment on which employment depends.

While the unions initially seemed to be trying to substitute for parties, the approach as it was subsequently developed cannot be interpreted simply as an alternative to action aimed at creating the political conditions for changing government policy. For one thing, the limits of a strategy of investment control when the government proved unable or unwilling to counteract the depressive effects of the international economic crisis were recognised by the unions. Their sense of urgency about government policy was intensified by their perception of the risk of an authoritarian mobilisation in reaction to deepening governmental paralysis, posing a threat to democracy and with it their own existence. For another thing, analysis and formulation of demands concerning concrete means to cope with the structural problems of specific sectors and firms was understood by some as contributing to the political conditions for changing governmental policy. Union officials and members involved in the expanded collective bargaining process, in which affiliates of all confederations often engaged jointly, were expected to become increasingly aware of both the difficulty and the potential for solving the problems, and also the need for political change to realise that potential. Thus the process could mobilise support for political change in such a way as to strengthen interconfederal cohesion rather than threaten it.

Furthermore, the process could also strengthen the unions' position regardless of political outcomes. If the composition of government was changed by entry of the PCI in such a way as to make it more willing to carry out the role assigned to it in the unions' new model of development, the unions would be better equipped to participate in the prescribed planning, both in influencing the substance of the plans and securing the co-operation of their members. If the composition of the government remains unchanged, as it has, the unions would still be in a better position to defend their members' interests, both through the accumulated expertise of their negotiators and their ability to mobilise their members. Conceivably, this could make the Italian confederations the least vulnerable to falling hostage to political parties.

Whether this would in fact be the case is by no means clear. However, this strategic perspective would seem to be the most interesting to emerge in the West European labour movements. It seems to point in the direction in which the Swedish and British labour movements would have to go, and in which the Swedish unions have gone to some extent, to meet the strategic prerequisites for achieving implementation of the economic programme on which they and the Italian labour movements seemed to converge. If the British labour movement would regroup around such a programme in the future and if the seeds of 'Italianisation' in the French labour movement bear fruit, the expansion of union roles that has been taking place in Italy may constitute the main response of European unions to the slow down of growth in the OECD area. Of the labour movements we studied, this would leave the German one as the only exception to the trend. Are there circumstances in which it too might move in the same direction? We will not venture a prediction on this, nor on the likelihood of a continuation of the trend, or a return to it, in the labour movements where it has been discerned, but we will point to some of the factors which would seem to be decisive in determining what happens in the light of our discussion so far.

As we suggested earlier, the unions' economic diagnoses and prescriptions have not been altered much by the impact of the mid-1970s crisis. By and large, they continued to view the economy as operating in the same way, vulnerable to the same problems, and requiring the same solutions, as they had come to view it in the preceding years of the decade, which constituted varying degrees of change from their views during the earlier post-war period. The extent and timing of such modifications in their view occurring after the impact suggests that they were primarily responses to political events that redefined their strategic problems. So if we want to understand persistence or change in union strategic perspectives (and to anticipate the likelihood of either in the future), we should expect it to depend on how unions evaluate the political conditions for protecting or advancing the whole range of interests, which they believe to be at stake, and to which they attach varying relative weights, including organisational survival as well as broad goals concerning the economy's performance or transformation. This is hardly surprising, either on general theoretical grounds or on the basis of what we already knew about the relationships between the individual labour movements and their national political contexts, but what we have learned has reinforced this conviction.

An additional facet of the way in which the impact of economic conditions on union strategies is refracted through the prisms of their national political contexts is the almost exclusively inward looking direction of their strategic perspectives. Given the extent of international integration not only through trade but also the transnational organisation of production and finance, the profound changes in the international pattern of investment and production, and the strong international linkages shaping the mid-1970s crisis, it might have been expected that all this would loom large in the unions diagnoses and prescriptions. This is not so. It is true that the national economies' positions in the international system are seen as important in defining the economies' problems in all cases. Moreover, in the most open economies, Sweden and Italy, the unions see the main issue not as the need to adapt industrial structure to a changing international environment but as the way in which it is done. The need, and the issue, is seen similarly in Britain as well, but with much less unanimity. In Germany, of course, the need is seen and accepted as is the prevailing mode of adaptation, while the difficulties are not yet seen as critical. It is in France, the least open of the economies, that there is the greatest questioning of the need. Regardless of these differences, all the labour movements see the solutions to whatever problems result in essentially national terms, whatever the differences in the solutions—involving various mixes of preservation or transformation of the existing mixed economy in the process of adaptation to the international economy or withdrawal from it. Very little is proposed and less is done to alter the international economic environment, particularly insofar as union action across national borders is concerned. The obstacles are of course enormous: labour remains nation-bound at a time when capital is less so than ever, leaving unions at a serious strategic disadvantage.

This, finally, reinforces our impression of the weight of each national labour movement's specific historical legacy in shaping the trajectory of its development. Whether this has resulted in trajectories of change or continuity, along lines discussed earlier, it is clear that they have not been much deflected by the mid-1970s crisis. At the same time, the intersection of national trajectories and international crisis does seem to have accelerated change, perhaps even precipitating some change where continuity has prevailed, so the pattern of similarities and differences among the labour movements continues to be in flux. Perceiving themselves to be on the defensive in all cases, the labour movements may yet evolve strategies which enable them to meet the challenges they face in their respective national arenas with greater prospects for success, and which may have enough in common to enable them to do so in the international arena as well.

Power and Dissent: The Trade Unions in the Federal Republic of Germany Re-Examined

Andrei S. Markovits and Christopher S. Allen*

We propose to shed some light on social democracy's contradictory role in advanced capitalism by looking at West German trade unions, which are among the most social democratic structures in post WWII European history. The connection between social democracy and trade unions is crucial because in no country where a social democratic party has governed has it done so without a long symbiotic relationship with a social democratic trade union movement. Germany, as one of the most successful and influential advanced capitalist countries where the social democratic option has experienced one of its longest, most powerful and also most tragic histories within the past one hundred years, represents an important case in this crucial area of structural interaction. The trade unions, in turn, highlight the most salient contours of this ongoing process which, ultimately, is a manifestation of an arduous class struggle.

This class struggle, however, has not taken place at a constant tempo in postwar Germany. Working class opposition (or dissent) to capital (and, perhaps in some cases to the state) has, thus far, had two distinct periods since the late 1940s. In the first section of the paper we will outline how strong working class dissent waxed in the immediate postwar years, until the period between the currency reform of 1948 and the implementation of the *Betriebsverfassungsgesetz* (Works Constitution Law) in 1952. We will then show that working class and trade union dissent (or opposition to capital and state) waned drastically during the *Wirtschaftswunder* (economic miracle) years of the 1950s and 1960s. The second section of the paper (the period beginning in the late 1960s and the early 1970s) will show that dissent among the German working class has begun to rise again, examined notably through an analysis of the DGB, the German Trade Union Confederation. Whether, at this point, we are witnessing a transformation of the German unions from "reformist reforms" to "revolutionary reforms"[1] will be discussed in the conclusion.

*Respectively Department of Government, Wesleyan University and Department of Politics, Brandeis University. We would like to express our gratitude to Ms. Brigitte Bailey for her helpful assistance in collecting some of the material used in this paper. Markovits thankfully acknowledges the financial support of the Ford Foundation and a Wesleyan University travel grant. Allen gratefully appreciates the assistance of the Isaiah Leo Sharfman Fellowship granted by Brandeis University and the Research Assistantship with Markovits under the auspices of the Center for European Studies at Harvard University.

THE GERMAN TRADE UNIONS: *Ordnungsfaktor* OR *Gegenmacht*[2]

A. *The Unions' Political Posture from the late 1940s until the late 1960s: Opposition, Incrementalism, Collaboration*

A crucial concern is the absolute necessity of placing the German working class' political expression and aspirations in the very unique context of the post-WWII settlement. Thus, for example, the frequent comparisons[3] of the relative 'meekness' on the part of the German working class compared to the 'militancy' of the Italian, French and British are devoid of an important explanatory dimension if they neglect to account for the severe break between the SPD and KPD in Weimar, and the destruction of both, especially the latter, at the hands of Fascism which broke the continuity of a living Marxist tradition so prevalent in both France and Italy. In Great Britain, although the Communist Party has never been large, there has always been a strong and militant working class consciousness which was not distracted by national questions such as repeated defeats in war and the division of the country as in Germany.

Still, in the Federal Republic, militant opposition to the reconstruction of a capitalist market economy immediately after the war permeated not only large segments of the working class and its two major political institutions, the SPD and the DGB, but also considerable sectors of the CDU's Left, following the socially oriented tenets of the *Christliche Soziallehre*.[4]

Indeed, it was precisely the trade union movement which in its newly unified form—in marked contrast to the Weimar period's hostile divisions according to party allegiances—represented the most serious and viable challenge to the forces of capital. From 1946–1948, the trade unions took strong positions in opposition to capital such as calling for the nationalisation of major industries, full co-determination in all industries, and calling for vast social programmes to redistribute wealth and income. Such opposition to capital has not been duplicated in the history of the Federal Republic of Germany despite current evidence of increasing militancy.

A combination of global and domestic factors exogenous to the trade unions impeded a possible system-transformation in the early stages of the Federal Republic. These factors included:

1. The presence of the three western powers, among whom the United States' predominance gained proportionately with the intensification of the Cold War.[5]

2. The increasingly repressive regime in East Germany and the Soviet Union as negative models of socialism.[6]

3. The Marshall Plan ,which was undertaken not only to aid the devastated German population as a humanitarian gesture but to restore the productive German capitalist economy. It was also instituted to fashion both a political and ideological bulwark against communism and to create an economic trading partner with a lucrative market.

4. The currency reform of 1948, which—by discriminating against those with savings accounts in favour of owners of productive property—clearly reintroduced and reinforced a very inegalitarian class structure. Not surprisingly, it was the wealthy who were the first to benefit from the fruits of the economic miracle.

5. The *Wirtschaftswunder* (economic miracle), perhaps the most convincing restoration and reaffirmation of capital anywhere.

There was a substantial economic base after WWII upon which the recovery could be built. The loss of Germany's industrial capacity as a consequence of war-related destruction was not as large as had been commonly assumed,[7] but was sufficient to benefit from a massive infusion of capital in its modernisation vis-à-vis its major industrial competitors. Furthermore, Germany enjoyed the luxury of having almost no military expenditures.

Some of the German economic miracle's most important ingredients, however, stem from the labour side of the equation. Foremost in this context were the 12 million German expellees and refugees from Eastern Europe and East Germany who arrived in the Federal Republic during the sixteen years between the end of WWII and the construction of the Berlin Wall.[8]

Two additional consequences of this migration aided the development of the German economy: the availability of a large reservoir of labour which kept wages lower than those of Germany's major competitors, permitted a more explicit exploitation[9] and created a convenient labour market through the influx of a relatively large number of newcomers with highly specialised skills. It is in this framework that the first ten years of the *Wirtschaftswunder* were based on a highly labour-intensive production process, contrary to the commonly-held notion of the superiority of German technology due to unusually active capital investment. It was not until the early 1960s, following the depletion of this important labour pool, that German capital responded in a two-pronged fashion: increasing capital intensification in the form of rationalisation and the importation of foreign workers from Europe's peripheries, mainly Turkey, Greece, Yugoslavia, southern Italy, Spain and Portugal.[10]

The unions, of course, helped shape this process and in turn were shaped by it. They developed, to use Frank Parkin's terminology, a "subordinate" posture, i.e., an accommodating mechanism and *Weltanschauung* vis-à-vis the inequalities of capitalism.[11] We have already shown some of the exogenous factors which help account for the German unions' lack of militancy from the early 1950s until the late 1960s in the preceding pages. However, this alone does not explain why a union movement, which showed such strong opposition to capital in the late 1940s, became so accommodationist in the 1950s. To answer this question properly, it becomes necessary to outline some of the actual measures taken by the unions during this period as well as the unions' perceptions of their own actions.

Few countries represent such a contrast in style between continuity and change as the Federal Republic of Germany. Two over-riding themes characterise trade union politics throughout the post-WWII period: a sincere belief in and active support of democracy[12] and—partly in contradiction, partly as a consequence—an over-riding sense of order, peace, and calculable regularity accompanied by a strong decentralisation.

This dichotomy can also be seen in the organisational structure of the German unions which was established after the war. On the one hand, the union leaders sought to prevent the internecine political feuds along party lines which existed during the Weimar period by relying upon the strong centralising tendencies of the *Einheitsgewerkschaft* (Unitary Trade

Union Movement) and the *Industriegewerkschaft* (Unions Organised Industrially). The *Einheitsgewerkschaft* established a united movement separate from party politics. The DGB considers itself independent but not neutral in the context of German party politics. Although its leadership is close to the SPD, the DGB claims to represent *all workers* thereby justifying its claim of being above party politics and fully able to be devoted to the working class as a whole. The *Industriegewerkschaft* merely transposed the concept of unity from the societal onto the plant and company level. In the Federal Republic, the equation of 'one plant one union' has had an important effect on the structure of industrial relations.

On the other hand, there was also a strong decentralising tendency which saw considerable power delegated to the sixteen (seventeen from April 1978) constituent unions of the DGB. For instance, not only are the individual unions totally autonomous in terms of policy making and implementation— especially as far as the crucial realm of collective bargaining is concerned— but they are further subdivided by region and industrial specialisation. To complicate matters organisationally, both the DGB and the constituent unions have their own separate units from the federal level all the way down to the branches.

The DGB's Munich Programme of 1949 expressed the following require- ments for a successful democracy and, by implication, set the appropriate guidelines for union politics: (1) Guaranteed full employment for all; (2) Full co-determination of all employed people in every aspect of their existence; (3) Socialisation of all key industries (e.g., mining, steel, iron, and chemicals, plus credit institutions and banks); and (4) Social justice for all by redistribu- tion of the social product.[13]

However, this partly anti-capitalist stance of the late 1940s and early 1950s reflected in the radical language of the Munich *Grundsatzprogramm* (Basic Founding Programme) of 1949 gradually dissipated. Some of this dissipation was clearly due to the inability of the unions to mobilise enough power to counter the formidable exogenous forces mentioned earlier. A significant portion was also due to the union leadership's policies and tactical short- comings during the early 1950s. Some of the setbacks and shortcomings suffered by the DGB included: the passage of a less comprehensive *Montan- mitbestimmung* (Coal & Steel Co-determination) law in 1951 than the DGB had originally demanded, and of the *Betriebsverfassungsgesetz* which severely curtailed the unions' rights in organising at the plant level; though professing party political neutrality, their overly heavy and uncritical tactical alliance with and reliance on the SPD and the latter's parliamentary road to power and social change;[14] their unwillingness to broaden their organisational efforts to recruit 'democratic Communists' and 'socialist Christians' which would have enabled the DGB to mobilise on a broader front against the powers of capital;[15] and an inability to recognise that, when threatened by the conservative thrusts of capital, the most appropriate action would have been to counter this move strongly and not to modify its demands and expectations.[16] In modifying its demands and goals, the DGB moved continuously further away from the democratisation of society which it had originally held to be so essential a goal.

But since the union leadership perceived that militant action was not appropriate, there must have been very good reasons why this was the case. One obvious explanation is that the unions increasingly identified their fate with that of resurgent German capitalism. One can very easily draw the parallel between the unions' action during this period and the action of the German left between 1905 and 1917 as described by Carl Schorske.[17] It should be made clear that the German unions were not simply bought off by the fruits of the economic miracle (just as it is too much an over-simplification to state that the Social Democrats between 1905 and 1917 were bought off by the fruits of an ascendant German imperialism). Rather the unions (as well as the Social Democrats earlier in the century) made their decisions as part of an ongoing step-by-step process. The important point is that, once they took positions on a certain set of issues, they made it difficult for themselves to take subsequent action in directions they had previously considered and rejected. Therefore, once the unions decided to take an accommodationist position toward capital in not continuing to push for the kind of fundamental social change outlined in their Munich Programme of 1949, it became increasingly difficult, if not impossible, for them to return to a position of strong opposition in their relationship with capital during the 1950s.

Organisationally as well, the union movement began to change in a clear and perceptible way. The types of individuals who either became attracted to union work or continued with union work after the unions became less radical were different from the union militants of the late 1940s.[18] Once the unions lost the vision of the transformation of capitalism into socialism, they were increasingly less likely to attract and select people who shared this *Weltanschauung,* and more likely to employ union careerists and bureaucrats lacking a comparable commitment.

Thus it is not surprising to note the progression from the radical programme of Munich to the 1955 DGB *Aktionsprogramm* heralded as a pragmatic adaptation to changed conditions, to the 1963 *Grundsatzprogramm* drawn up in Dusseldorf, which finalised and codified the unions' deradicalisation. Dusseldorf was the unions' Bad Godesberg. It represented the ideological adaptation—and logical conclusion—to a continuous process. Since this process is so crucial toward explaining the unions' movement from a *Gegenmacht* to an *Ordnungsfaktor,* it will be examined in three crucial areas, the union movements' relations with: the working class, capital and the state.

Union-Working Class Relations. There is very little doubt that the unions see themselves as the genuine all-encompassing representatives of the entire German working class, and *not only* the organised workers, comprising about 7.5 million people, i.e. 34 per cent of the German work force.[19] Following their Marxist heritage—in contrast with the business unionism of most American unions—German unions always speak in the name of and for German workers. This concept is partly responsible for the fact that German unions did not demand closed shop arrangements and do not mind when non-unionised workers are equally the beneficiaries of union-led struggles; while most workers also see the unions as the legitimate and effective representatives of the working class.[20]

Structurally the *Einheitsgewerkschaft* and the *Industriegewerkschaft* obviate divisions along party lines and unite workers performing different jobs, e.g. blue and white collar. The unions' services to the working class could best be characterised by the proto-typical social democratic tandem: hard-nosed bread-and-butter bargaining resulting in incremental material gains, and the securing of a more humane social existence in the form of various non-material benefits.

However, two problem areas have marred the otherwise successful relationship between the unions and the working class: one, upward directed, namely the relationship of the DGB toward the SPD; the other, downward directed, namely the complex relationship between the unions and the *Betriebsräte* (works councils). There is very little doubt as to the close ties between the DGB and SPD, despite the DGB's *parteipolitische Unabhängigkeit* (independence of political parties). This is manifested in an historical bond of common tradition, a high overlap of personnel on the leadership level, and a similar outlook of the leadership and membership.[21] This symbiotic relationship between the DGB and the SPD has benefited both; yet, one could argue that the DGB's total submission to the SPD in terms of political and macro-economic questions not only hampered its own organisational decision making but played an important role in the deradicalisation of the German working class. For once the unions, following the SPD, lost the radical vision of the transformation of capitalism into socialism and took as their primary vision the securing of material benefits for their members within the framework of capitalism, the primary activity became the fostering of the DGB itself, the organisation that could best fulfil these changed requirements. Even if the unions' aims still were the radical transformation of society, the presence of a strong organisation would obviously have been a crucial necessity; but once the option of a radical transformation had disappeared, the DGB's primary goal became its own institutional self-preservation within the framework of a capitalist society. Therefore, when faced with a choice between daringly pushing forward increased working class demands or maintaining its present organisational position, the latter course was more often followed. Denied a vehicle for the expression of the goal of fundamental social change, it is thus not surprising that the working class became much less radical.

As to the role of the second problem area, the works councils have helped capital keep the unions from entering the immediate day-to-day affairs of workers on the plant level, thereby weakening working class unity and enhancing management control. The unions moved away from a goal of societal transformation toward one of institutional self-preservation and securing of material benefits. Concomitantly it is not unusual to witness the works councils also pursuing a narrower focus by often identifying more with the issues concerning one particular plant than with those regarding the trade unions or the working class at large.

Union-Capital Relations. Initially openly hostile, culminating in the 1951–52 strike waves across the country, these relations became co-operatively antagonistic. The institutional basis of discourse was anchored in the mutual respect of *Tarifautonomie* (bargaining autonomy) which derives from the Basic Law of 1949 (the Federal Republic's Constitution) and stipulates non-interference by either party in the other's domain during the bargaining process. Most importantly, the unions' major strategy vis-à-vis capital lay in their strong conviction of the benefits of co-determination, which has been a unique German attempt to deal with problems for the working class caused by advanced capitalism.[22] *Mitbestimmung* was thought to be (in the late 1940s) a way to transform German society radically. But when implemented in 1951 in the coal and steel industries (where labour had one less than 50 per cent of the members on the Supervisory Board of Directors) and in 1952 in other industries (where labour had only one-third representation on the Boards),[23] it became more a mechanism for structural integration of the German working class than for radical social change. However, by this time the working class had become less radical and *Mitbestimmung* was perceived to provide some worthwhile though not fundamental changes for the unions. It is only later, in the 1970s, that dissent over the implementation of *Mitbestimmung* begins to rise once again.

Union-State Relations. This is the most complex and intricate of the three. In a sense, the union leadership since the days of the Weimar Republic saw the state as either its ally against capital or as a neutral arbiter in the class struggle.[24] This factor must also be seen as contributing to the stifling of German working class militancy. At important historical junctures the unions' attitude toward the state has acted as a brake on segments of the working class who felt that the state would be able to provide the fruits which could not be obtained via militant class conflict. The unions have constantly looked to the state for help, be it in terms of Keynesian-type conjunctural policies, or legal action, both from the courts and the legislature. The state, in a sense, has very much remained the *Obrigkeitsstaat* (a society in which the concept of the state's authority is paramount) of earlier days. Thus, one could conclude that, whereas the unions are certainly antagonistic vis-à-vis capital, they are not vis-à-vis the state. They are *staatstreu* (loyal to the state). They act as if they do not understand that the state in capitalism is by necessity a capitalist state.

This identification with the state as a beneficial—or at least neutral—structure has been, of course, enhanced by the SPD's position in power since 1969. However, the combination of the SPD's hold on power for almost a decade, the end of the economic miracle, and the anti-radical decrees have all caused this *staatstreu* attitude (and, by implication, the present concept of German social democracy) to be re-evaluated by left-wing individuals in general and by some union members in particular.

B.   *The Union Movement in the 1970s: Inept Colossus or Sole Bastion of Democracy?*

The late 1960s brought substantial changes to the political climate of the Federal Republic, as to so many other advanced industrial countries. An important harbinger heralding a more problematic future for relations between labour and capital was the Federal Republic's first post-WWII recession in 1966/67 in which the actual GNP declined in real terms.[25]

Just as the 'end of ideology' seemed to reach its epitome in the Grand
Coalition between the CDU and the SPD, and in the neo-corporatist
arrangement of 'concerted action'—a response, incidentally, to the economic
crisis of 1966/67—events proved the end of ideology's evanescent nature.
Led by students at many German universities, the so-called extra-parlia-
mentary opposition (APO) shattered the harmonious complacency of
German public life. Providing a comprehensive critique in theory and
practice of the interdependent deficiencies inherent in advanced capitalism,
few established institutions of the Federal Republic remained unscathed.
This did not only include the state bureaucracy, political parties, universities
and the media, but also the unions. It is partly in this context that one has
to view the significance of the unions' partial alliance with the students
against the powers that be in opposing the emergency laws, one of the
first unconcealed steps of the West German state to control resurgent
political dissent. Similarly, the September strikes of 1969 followed the
pattern of a renewed critical stance on the part of the unions vis-à-vis
capital. These events were characterised by overt opposition and dissent,
long absent from the German political economy.

The first major and relatively long-lasting (from the 2 to 19 September
1969) strikes in the Federal Republic since the strikes of 1951 in favour
of *Montanmitbestimmung,* the September strikes encompassed most regions
of the country. Although purely defensive in character—in the sense that
the strikes were conducted merely to regain lost ground in wages—the
involvement of various branches of mining and metal industries lent it
additional weight. The strikes should be regarded as a watershed in the
post-WWII relations between labour and capital, when levels of opposition
and dissent became clearly visible again, though not of a fundamentally
system-threatening nature.

To paraphrase the analysis of the strikes by a group of German scholars:
the German working class moved from being of the system to being in it.[26]
This apt characterisation received added dimension throughout the early
1970s and culminated in a renewed strike wave in 1973, this time including
public employees, as well as workers in growth industries such as chemicals
and electronics. 1973, of course, represented "the great divide" so well
named by Erhard Eppler, a leading member of the SPD, not only for
German industrial relations but for the entire capitalist world economy.
Things would never be the same again.

The world-wide crisis of capitalism, culminating in the most severe
recession (1974/75) since the Great Depression of the 1930s, did not spare
the Federal Republic. The breakdown of the Bretton Woods monetary
system, its replacement by an unpredictable free currency market subject
to massive speculations, and the oil crisis with its aftermath, contributed
to an end to at least the more consensual aspects of capital-labour relations.
Stagflation, hitherto largely unknown to Germans, became a continuous
problem of their daily lives. Over one million unemployed—about 4 per
cent of the labour force—have persisted since 1974/75, an unparalleled
longevity in the history of the Federal Republic. Things, in a word, have
become different between labour and capital. Class lines are more pro-

nounced, the tone of discourse is more acerbic, strikes and lockouts have increased, in short the class struggle has become more manifest; and indeed it may have entered a new phase in post-WWII German history. How have the unions perceived this new situation? What issues do they regard as salient; and what do they believe are the major causes? What policy responses and strategies if any, do the unions have?

It is important to understand that the attitudes and positions of the German unions vis-à-vis such issues as the most pressing contemporary problems, their main causes, and overall implications are far from consistent. Indeed they change quite frequently though not randomly; rather they change in connection with the respective union's position in the political economy. The same pertains to strategies which, although more short term oriented, are still far from following a clear and compelling line. Nevertheless, there are some overall concepts concerning all of the above which define the current existence of the German labour movement during a time of increasing class struggle, even rank and file militancy. The 1978/79 strikes, culminating in the bitter steel and iron workers strike predominantly in North Rhine-Westphalia (from November 28, 1978 to January 6, 1979) involving nearly 100,000 workers, may represent a transitional phase in the hitherto antagonistic yet co-operative relationship between labour and capital.

The DGB's Major Concerns. The major problems for the DGB as repeatedly stated in all publications over the last few years and re-emphasised during the 11th Ordinary Federal Congress held at Hamburg in May, 1978,[27] are: unemployment; rationalisation; working conditions; capital export; qualitative growth; new forms of political repression in the larger context of the anti-terrorist laws; exacerbation of the class struggle on the part of the employers by the increasing use of lockouts; and the legalisation of class conflict by capital's use of the courts in contesting the *Mitbestimmung* Law of 1976. The strong stands which the DGB has taken on these issues are indicative of the seriousness with which it views them and represents a major cause for the DGB's increasingly dissenting position vis-à-vis capital.

The reasons for the crisis are clear as far as the DGB is concerned. Capital, which the DGB perceives as stronger and, by definition, in an advantageous position, is systematically trying to weaken—possibly even destroy—labour. The world crisis of 1974/75, which the DGB analyses as largely exogenous to the German political economy, gave capital an excellent opportunity to weaken the German labour movement.

(a) Ideologically, this is done on all fronts by constantly talking of a trade union state and conjuring up the old fear of a red menace; a process wherein the current anti-terrorist hysteria in the Federal Republic comes to capital's aid.

(b) Politically, by using the CDU/CSU—though *not* the SPD—and the FDP (to a lesser degree), the media, parts of academia and research organisations such as the *Sachverständigenrat* ('Five Wise Men', the rough German equivalent to the American Council of Economic Advisers) and most recently the courts. Capital also will use the state for this purpose, but usually in more covert ways.

(c) In the labour market, by maintaining unemployment and keeping wages down, and by rationalising entire industries out of existence.

(d) In investment, by either going abroad or investing in labour saving equipment.

(e) In *Konjunkturpolitik* (short-term demand management), again the culprit is capital alone, not the state, which by itself is not sufficient to solve the crisis; and in which case capital's interests lie only in gaining tax cuts, the benefits of which will simply be invested in the above-mentioned manner.

(f) In the ramifications of the international monetary system in which, despite the revaluation of the Deutschemark, German exports boomed due largely to: the reliability of German products, the relative price inelasticity of many industrial products, and the higher inflation in most recipient countries trading with Germany. The windfall profits emanating from the revaluation of the Deutschmark were not passed on in wages, if anything they could be seen as profit-augmenting.

What are the specific issues which are of the greatest concern to the DGB?

(1) *Unemployment:* This is by far the key problem for the DGB, especially since, for the fifth year in a row, the figures hovered above the one million mark, about 4 per cent of the German labour force. Simply stated, capital argues that the way out of the crisis is easy: wage restraints= higher profits=more investments=more employment, which will satisfy everyone since labour's main complaint rests on the high level of unemployment. The DGB's proposal, not surprisingly, is the exact opposite: wage increases and more jobs=higher consumption=higher profits=more investment.[28]

The DGB feels that private demand is the main support of the economy and points out that workers are the largest group of consumers. Higher wages to workers, therefore, far from being detrimental to growth, would stimulate it. The DGB is critical of capital's plans—apart from the obvious reasons—because it argues that capital does nothing to increase capacity utilisation as capital claims it does. In numerous studies, the DGB is intent on showing how capital's profits continue to increase without any effects on productive growth: profits are used for rationalisation, for deposits in foreign bank accounts and investments in foreign countries.[29]

The question of capacity underutilisation is crucial because it is directly related to rationalisation and taken together both act as perpetuators of unemployment. The DGB proposal to overcome this calls for a reduction of work time to a 35 hour week with no reduction in pay, extended vacations of up to six weeks, a tenth year of compulsory education, early retirement and better protection for workers against rationalisation, as the number of jobs lost due to rationalisation since 1973 is between 1.3 and 1.8 million.[30]

The results of this rationalisation on levels of production efficiency are instructive; in 1976 German industry produced 7.2 per cent more goods with 2.5 per cent less labour yielding approximately 10 per cent higher output per worker. This process, and the consequential unemployment, become the primary justification for shortening work time as the DGB states that, in the past sixteen years, the goods production of the German economy has doubled while the work input has dropped concomitantly from 56 to 46 billion week/hours. Therefore, the DGB holds that if it had not been able to reduce the work week from 48 to 40 hours in the early 1960s, there would be mass unemployment now.[31]

In addition to all the above measures to counter unemployment, the DGB relies very much on state intervention on a massive scale to expand demand and thereby create jobs. One article citing a study from a very prestigious economic research institute shows that without state intervention on a massive scale there will be over two million unemployed by 1985. State investment to prevent this could cost anywhere from DM 380 billion to DM 600 billion. The DGB is fully aware of the fact that this type of *Konjunkturpolitik* would meet with considerable resistance in many quarters due to the already high levels of public deficits. It counters its own worries, however, with the fact that this type of state investment would be tantamount to a loan, a good investment in fact, since the public would get it all back in taxes and social expenditures, rather than being stuck with having to pay unemployment compensation and welfare benefits.[32]

(2) *Rationalisation:* As already obvious from the previous discussion of unemployment, this problem has gripped the unions, especially over the last two years. The areas mostly affected by this are printing, office work (especially worrisome to the public employees union), chemicals and electronics. Countless articles, cartoons and back covers of union publications convey the great preoccupation of the unions with this development. When talking about word processors, micro-computers and calculators, the unions describe them literally and in English as 'job-killers.'[33]

This intensified rationalisation introduces an additional form of unemployment to the already existing conjunctural and structural ones, best denoted by the term technological.[34] Whereas the causes for the first are typically sluggish or deficient growth leading to unused capacity, and for the second a badly functioning co-ordination between the demanded job/skill qualifications and the existent supply in the labour market, technological unemployment is a new phenomenon, affecting hitherto highly employable groups such as white collar employees and university-trained personnel. The unions admit to not having devoted sufficient time to this phenomenon in the past. As far as strategies countering this development are concerned, the unions seem to think that this being an unconventional form of unemployment, it would require an unconventional remedy to cure the illness: shortening of work time, job sharing, and the de-privatisation (or socialisation) of all burdens due to rationalisation.

Yet, the DGB always goes to great length to assure the public that the German labour movement is not made up of machine-smashers and various other crypto-Luddite elements. Indeed, it has always welcomed technical changes and technological innovations, when they have benefited the workers.

> In the past the DGB has welcomed the results of rationalisation and technical change insofar as it was ensured that, by raising work productivity, it was possible to improve workers' social conditions

and no negative effects occurred at their expense . . . Should those in political responsibility fail to do away with mass unemployment the trade union position on rationalisation and technical change must be critically rethought.[35]

(3) *Capital Export:* This represents a very serious problem to which the unions have no immediate answer save for demanding that the state intervene in some fashion. Numerous articles point out the demise of entire industries due to German capital's flight abroad, including the United States. Certain aspects of neo-protectionism are unquestionably discernible in this. With good reason: whereas there were only 455,000 people employed in German companies abroad in 1966, the figure reached over 1.5 million by 1975. For every 100 domestic jobs in processing industries, there were 5 abroad in 1966; there were 20 by 1975.[36]

The only comprehensive attempt to find an answer to this problem can be found in an article by Karl Buschmann,[37] the president of the *Textil-Bekleidung* (textile-clothing) union, probably the hardest hit by capital export. He argues that Ricardo's law of comparative costs is used by capital of the First World to exploit labour in both the First and Third Worlds and pit them against each other in a desperate battle for jobs. His solutions seem a positive-sum strategy for everyone involved: increasing wages for the workers in the Third World, thereby decreasing their misery and exploitation *and* making them consumers of the products they currently produce for the First World. This would decrease the pressure for the industrial countries to import the products from the Third World, thereby saving the jobs of First World workers.

(4) *Lockouts:* Often used in the Weimar Republic as a weapon against labour, this particular measure has been deployed only from time to time in the Federal Republic until recently. Capital resorted to this measure three times in 1978/79—in the cases of the *IG Druck und Papier* and *IG Metall* strikes of spring 1978 and the *IG Metall* strike of winter 1978/79—in each case with determination, fanfare, and at the very beginning of the respective conflicts. This has clearly exacerbated class conflict, giving it a unique German twist, since nowhere else in Europe's recent past has this measure been used by capital with such vigour and determination. Indeed, that is one of labour's major arguments in underscoring the reactionary character of German capital. Again, however, there has been no mention of the state which, in this case, is unquestionably involved in a direct manner through legal and constitutional implications.

The problem is clearly political. It seems that capital is trying to use the current crisis to weaken labour by draining its strike funds, depriving workers of their livelihood and generally demoralising them. Capital argues that the lockout is its equivalent to labour's strike. This is substantiated by the ambiguities of the Basic Law, the Federal Republic's constitution, which mentions neither the right to strike nor the right to lock out but merely refers to the above-mentioned *Tarifautonomie* and *Koalitionsfreiheit* which gives each party the right to form coalitions and maintain non-interference and total autonomy in the bargaining process.

F

Labour argues that the lockout can never be the equivalent to the strike in a situation where capital owns the means of production and determines conditions in the best of times. Whereas the strike is labour's only weapon, the lockout is capital's most cynical in an inherently unequal relationship. The unions obtained some important support in their determined fight against lockouts: the SPD, Willy Brandt and a labour court which, in late 1978, held lockouts to be illegal. The issue, far from resolved, is clearly of central concern to the unions.

THE UNIONS' POSITION: A CRUCIAL WEAKNESS

Thus far we have examined the unions' primary concerns as well as their strategies for addressing them. The following pages will analyse whether or not the unions' strategies and tactics are capable of solving the problems which the unions have identified as being crucial, i.e. unemployment, rationalisation, capital export and lockouts. In the unions' view, the resolution of these problems would produce qualitative economic growth benefiting the working class first and foremost. However, the unions' programme contains one crucial weakness, the ramifications of which lead to a larger theoretical problem.

The keystone of the unions' present strategy lies in their increased employment/consumption-led model of economic recovery (in opposition to capital's plan of a profit-led growth). This strategy's importance to the unions is such that it is considered the *sine qua non* for the solution of all previously outlined issues. The DGB holds that: (a) increased employment would create higher demand, in turn fostering greater economic growth; (b) this process would reduce the pressure for rationalisation because it would eliminate its major cause, low profits; and (c) by improving profit levels in Germany, this process would also diminish the need for capital export since this would result in a higher rate of return on domestic investment for capital. In short, the DGB maintains that benefits applied directly to the working class would create the conditions for both a more humane society and an improved economy, hence qualitative economic growth.

At first glance, this programme seems eminently reasonable. However one major flaw, of which the unions seem unaware, has not gone unnoticed by capital. The latter has been quick to point out—and in no uncertain terms—that the implementation of this union-devised strategy would be highly inflationary to the German economy.[38] Capital's assessment is accurate since this programme would start a chain of consequences before increased employment and higher wages could lead to improved economic conditions.

The first consequence would entail a tightening of the labour market which, by itself, would drive up wages. The second would be the additional effect higher wage settlements would have on reducing profit levels. In this context, the unions have neglected a key point, namely capital's response of price increases. In a monopolistic/oligopolistic economy, little built-in pressure exists forcing capital to keep price levels low. Thus, at a crucial juncture, the unions' plan would founder because capital's control of the production and pricing process would prevent the kind of national redistribution of income which is essential to the unions' goal of qualitative economic growth. The unions would simply play a game in which, as soon as they pulled even, capital would once again spring ahead.

The larger theoretical problem here is one of control. None of the unions' official programmes, demands and analyses seriously deal with this issue. At best, only certain segments of the rank and file articulate this point. Even the unions' long standing goal of full parity *Mitbestimmung* in all firms with more than 2,000 employees does not aim at controlling the firm or the economy, since the deciding vote in any deadlock would be cast by a board member appointed by capital. The unions' shortcomings regarding the issue of control are visible in a number of areas.

If one divided all the unions' programmes and demands into offensive and defensive categories, most would fall within the latter. In a crucial sense, even the Janus-like depiction of the trade unions—*Ordnungsfaktor* or *Gegenmacht*—fails to address the issue of control. The term *Gegenmacht* means literally counter power; any countervailing power, however, can only exist in relation to a previously established power, in this case that of capital. Thus by not dealing with the issue of control, the unions necessarily relegate themselves to a structurally subservient position in capitalism before they even began to act as a *Gegenmacht*.

Not even the unions' demand for jobs, their most important concern, raises the issue of control. By not tackling this point, the unions must simply take the jobs which are given to them by capital.[39] In so doing, they give up the opportunity to decide important issues such as what goods are produced, which are marketed (and how), where investment will take place, and for what purpose. Thus important decisions regarding the quality of life, about which the unions care so deeply, are made for them by individuals whose primary goals are the immediate amassing of profits as well as the maintenance of a structure and climate which will insure this capability in the future.

An example of this problem is provided by the unions' attitude regarding nuclear power. As already mentioned, the unions are largely in favour of the continued construction of nuclear power plants. A good illustration of their reasoning can be seen in an article by the IG Chemie Chairman, stating that due to coal's position as Germany's sole indigenous energy source, it becomes necessary to develop alternate forms of energy.[40] The shortcoming of this position centres around the absence of an analysis as to who exactly decides what these sources will be and how they will be developed. By never posing these fundamental questions the unions are inadvertently channelled into a structural position favouring the deployment of nuclear power plants. The reasoning of atomic energy=more growth= more jobs pivots totally around the latter factor, over which the unions have no influence.

Rationalisation poses another theoretical problem in the context of control. Although not opposed to technological change "in principle", the DGB clearly states that it favours innovation "which has benefited the workers." However, since most technological change does not centre

primarily around the concerns of workers, it is not surprising that the
unions are generally distrustful of rationalisation in a fundamental sense.
Thus the primary reason for the unions' suspicious attitude toward rationalisation and innovation lies in their inability to view and shape the changes
that take place. They are only left to fight a defensive battle for jobs, the
requirements of which are determined elsewhere.

A final example of this phenomenon can be seen in the settlement of the
steel strike which took place during the winter of 1978–79. Capital, unlike
the unions, showed a heightened awareness of the need for control. It was
willing to trade off higher salaries and as much as six weeks of holiday
rather than withstand the actual and psychological threat to its prerogatives
which the implementation of the 35 hour work week would have represented.
That capital's class consciousness and strategic awareness concerning its
role in German industrial relations had very tangible manifestations
became public knowledge within one week of the conclusion of the iron
and steel strike. Reports by the conservative business daily *Handelsblatt*
and the Left-inclined *Frankfurter Rundschau* on January 15, 1979 disclosed
the existence of a *Tabu Katalog*. Therein the *Bundesvereinigung der Arbeit-
geberverbände* (one of the three major Federal Employers Associations)
or BDA laid down strict guidelines, particularly concerning working
conditions, work time and issues of control which all its constituent members
had to follow. The unions' reaction was swift. Viewed as "class war from
above," by various DGB and SPD leaders, DGB Chairman Heinz Vetter
warned of the possibility of an imminent "total confrontation" between
labour and capital.[41] However, unless the unions learn a lesson from this
'taboo catalogue' and develop offensive strategies to accompany their
present defensive ones, it is unlikely that they will succeed in implementing
the goals which they have so boldly proclaimed. Their dissent and opposition
to capital must not be haphazard; rather it must be carefully planned
and executed as well as be part of a strategy with long term goals. Leo
Panitch[42] maintains that, for workers to achieve fundamental change, they
must move beyond strategies such as *Mitbestimmung* which see participation
as an end in itself. In contrast they must view movements for workers'
control as a means (via actual practice) to develop the kinds of working
class action and consciousness necessary for fundamental structural change.
Among these would be strategies to direct the production and marketing
of goods as well as the purpose and location of investment. Thus the struggle
for control cannot be obtained merely by the passing of a law in the
Bundestag. Authentic control is only realised when deciding essential
day-to-day issues. Whether the unions will be able to develop such strategies
remains an open question, the answer to which will be a major determinant
of the unions' success in the immediate future.

CONCLUSION

The German labour movement is currently at an important crossroad.
For the first time in its history it may have the opportunity to combine
the increasing welfare of its members with an active and realistic political

challenge to the existing system, thereby enhancing German democracy in the process. This is a momentous occasion in the context of the history of the German working class. Indeed, it represents very much a synthesis of its past and its hopes for the future, which has hitherto remained elusive. Whereas the period until 1945 left both goals largely unfulfilled, the post-WWII era succeeded in providing some important material and moral gains without, however, a concomitant decrease in the unequal power relationships inherent in a capitalist society. In short, until the early 1970s the German working class was better off in absolute terms than ever before in its history.

However, the present crisis of the world and German economies has reduced this upward trajectory of material benefits. More significantly, it has also highlighted to the German labour movement two crucial and inter-dependent political factors: that the present welfare of the German working class, so much taken for granted, is based on a continuous struggle and indeed may be lost again; and that material welfare without social equality is vacuous at best. The objective conditions of an irreversible end to the *Wirtschaftswunder* and the waning of the WWII experience, combined with the unique events of its aftermath, contribute to a change in the political discourse and social climate of the Federal Republic. The honeymoon is over, as are special relationships and the much-admired *Burgfrieden* (social peace) between labour and capital. The lines are drawn as a discussion of issues such as rationalisation, unemployment, lockouts and the controversy over the 1976 *Mitbestimmung* law has indicated in this paper. Problems barely mentioned in this study and of far-ranging significance such as the *Radikalenerlass* (Radicals Decree)—*Berufsverbot* (employment ban), the use of sophisticated electronic technology in gathering information, and the state's recent repressive attitude in general—backed by powerful groups and institutions in society—support this assessment.

Yet Bonn is not Weimar, either in domestic or foreign affairs. Rather it is precisely due to a strong liberal bourgeois democracy that a fascist solution to the crisis is highly unlikely. Nor is there a realistic possibility of an escape via the Soviet-East German model of socialism.

Thus, two options remain: either a continuation of the muddling through of the past without, however, the accompanying material rewards that characterised a unique period in the development of Germany; or the formation of an active coalition of all progressive forces in German society in quest of the establishment of a democratisation and control of all aspects of German life through a process of daily political struggle. It is in this context that the German labour unions would have to play a leading institutional, political and moral role toward the transformation of present German society.

One theme of our paper maintains that the first option contains a number of pitfalls which make the second the only viable direction for the unions to take. The former is only possible under a prosperous economy able to provide sufficient benefits to satisfy most working class demands. It is rather uncertain whether even the German economy is capable of muddling through in a sustained fashion. Rank and file dissent, already of growing significance in the German labour movement, may well represent a challenge to the unions' defensive posture in a contracting economy. Therefore the unions must retain the possibility and capability of formulating and implementing offensive measures to secure qualitative social change. Failure to do so could result in a foreclosure of certain opportunities now present for the unions, especially if capital and the state were to pursue harsher retrenchment measures. Eventually such a defensive strategy could possibly even lead to a situation in which the relinquishing by the unions of previously attained rights become commonplace to German industrial conflict, much as they have in the weakened American union movement.

The key, then, becomes the second option, the formation of a progressive coalition to channel dissent and opposition, and to push for fundamental social change. It is quite clear to us that without the unions' active engagement on all levels of this endeavour, the transformation of present German society will remain incomplete, possibly doomed to failure. We believe that numerous present factors concerning both the German political economy and the unions' recent development embody elements with a potential for fundamental structural change. Whether the German labour movement will seize the opportunity, thereby contributing to the process of transforming social democracy into democratic socialism, only time will tell.

NOTES

1. Andre Gorz, *Strategy for Labor* (Boston: Beacon Press, 1967), pp. 4–5.
2. These two German terms, 'stabilizing factor' and 'counter power', respectively, are widely used by the unions themselves and especially within the vast German literature on this topic.
3. Michael Shalev, 'Lies, Damned Lies and Strike Statistics: The Measurement of Trends in Industrial Conflict' in Alessandro Pizzorno and Colin Crouch, eds., *The Resurgence of Class Conflict in Western Europe Since 1968* (New York: Holmes & Meier, 1978), pp. 1–19.
4. The Ahlener Programme of the CDU, when viewed through the prism of the conservative German Christian Democracy of the 1960s and 1970s, is quite a remarkable document in that it offered proposals for far-reaching social change which represented a considerable threat to the prerogatives of capital. See Helga Grebing, *Geschichte der deutschen Arbeiterbewegung: Ein Uberblick,* 2nd ed. (München: Nymphenburger Verlagshandlung, 1966); Hans Limmer, *Die deutsche Gewerkschaftsbewegung* (München: Günter Olzog Verlag, 1970); and Joachim Bergmann, Otto Jacobi and Walter Muller-Jentsch, *Gewerkschaften in der Bundesrepublik* (Frankfurt am Main: Europäische Verlagsanstalt, 1975).
5. The pervasive role of the Americans—in notable opposition to the British, whose Labour government at the time viewed the formation of an activist labour movement with some benevolence, if not outright enthusiasm—in preventing any radicalisation of the German unions is well documented. See Eberhard Schmidt, *Die verhinderte Neuordnung 1945–1952* (Frankfurt am Main: Europäische Verlagsanstalt, 1970); Theo Pirker, *Die blinde Macht Vol. 1* (München: Mercator Verlag, 1960). American unions played some direct as well as indirect roles in this intervention. On the latter point, see Victor Agartz, *Gewerkschaft und Arbeiterklasse* (München: C. Trikont-Verlag, 1971).
6. Heinz Abosch *The Menace of the Miracle* (New York: Monthly Review Press, 1963).
7. Guido Goldman, 'The German Political System' in S. Beer and A. Ulam, eds., *Patterns of Government* (New York: Random House, 1976), p. 566. See also Günter

Minnerup, 'The *Bundesrepublik* Today,' *New Left Review*, No. 99 (Sept.–Oct. 1976) p. 14.

8. Charles Kindleberger sees this migration as the foremost factor in Germany's post WWII economic miracle. See his *Europe's Postwar Growth: The Role of Labor Supply* (Cambridge: Harvard University Press, 1967).

9. Until 1960, average German wages were less than 30% of current levels, see *OECD— Germany—1978,* Annexe III. Even allowing for the mild German inflation levels since that time, this is still a startling figure. In fact, it was only in 1964 that the gross hourly wages of male workers surpassed DM 4 per hour—1963, DM 3.79 and 1964, DM 4.19. See Dresdner Bank, *Statistical Survey,* November 1977. Furthermore, a 50 hour work week remained the average until the late 1950s, see Minnerup, 'The *Bundesrepublik* Today', *op. cit.*

10. See for example Andrei S. Markovits and Samantha Kazarinov, 'Class Conflict, Capitalism and Social Democracy: The Case of Migrant Workers in the Federal Republic of Germany,' *Comparative Politics* (April 1978), pp. 372–391.

11. Frank Parkin, *Class, Inequality and Political Order* (New York: Praeger, 1971). See also Michael Szeplabi, *Das Gesellschaftsbild der Gewerkschaften* (Stuttgart: Ferdinand Enke Verlag, 1973), pp. 101–107.

12. For a recent reaffirmation of the unions' commitment to democracy throughout the Federal Republic's thirty year history, see especially President Walter Scheel's address to the DGB Congress in May 1978 wherein he repeatedly emphasised the unions' unrivalled democratic engagement in day-to-day politics; 'Bundespräsident Scheel: Gewerkschaften sind ein mächtiges Bollwerk der Demokratie,' *Die Quelle* (June 1978), p. 332.

13. Bernd Otto, *Die Gewerkschaftsbewegung in Deutschland* (Cologne: Bund Verlag, 1975), pp. 107–109.

14. See E. Schmidt *Die verhinderte, op. cit.,* Parts I and III.

15. William D. Graf, *The German Left Since 1945* (Cambridge: The Oleander Press, 1976), Chapter 3.

16. See Pirker, *Die blinde Macht, op. cit.,* especially Vol. 1, Chapter 6.

17. Carl E. Schorske, *German Social Democracy: 1905–1917* (Princeton: Princeton University Press, 1955).

18. See Abosch, *The Menace, op. cit.,* Chapter 7.

19. See *DGB Report,* No. 11–1, 1978, p. 15.

20. See 'Gewerkschaftsbarometer 1978 bestätigt die gewerkschaftliche Politik.' *Die Quelle* (June 1978), pp. 389–392.

21. See Grebing, *Geschichte, op. cit.,* especially p. 279.

22. For a thorough exposition of all implications on *Mitbestimmung,* see Alfred Diamant, 'Democratizing the Workplace: The Myth and Reality of *Mitbestimmung* in the Federal Republic of Germany,' Paper presented at the APSA Annual Meeting, Chicago: September, 1976. The literature on every aspect of *Mitbestimmung* is vast. For social scientists, the works of Heinz Hartmann and Peter Velte are very informative. For an excellent collection of critical essays on *Mitbestimmung,* see Frank Deppe, Jutta von Freyberg, Christof Kievenheim, Regine Meyer and Frank Werkmeister, *Kritik der Mitbestimmung: Partnerschaft oder Klassenkampf* (Frankfurt am Main, Edition Suhrkamp, 1973).

23. James Furlong, *Labor in the Boardroom* (New York: Dow-Jones Publishers, 1977).

24. For an excellent discussion of this point, see Volker Bahl, 'Lohnverhandlungssystem der Weimarer Republik—Von der Schlichtungsverordnung zum Ruhreisenstreit: Verbandsautonomie oder staatliche Verbandsgarantie?' *Gewerkschaftliche Monatshefte* (July 1978), pp. 397–411.

25. The GNP's decline was —0.1% after having grown an average of 6.6% per year since 1951. The more narrowly measured industrial production also declined for the first time by —2.8% after averaging 7.7% increases since 1951. See Dresdner Bank, *Statistical Survey,* November 1977.

26. Michael Schumann, Frank Gerlach, Albert Gschlössl and Petra Millhöfer, *Am Beispiel der Septemberstreiks: Anfang der Rekonstruktionsperiode der Arbeiterklasse*? (Frankfurt am Main: Europäische Verlagsanstalt, 1971). See section A, pp. 1–14.

27. The following sources contain information concerning the 11th Ordinary Congress

of the DGB of May, 1978: *Die Quelle,* May and June 1978; *DGB Report,* Vol. 14, No. 3, 1978: and Heinz O. Vetter, 'Mit dem Rücken zur Wand?' *Gewerkschaftliche Monatshefte,* April 1978, pp. 193–202.

28. For a clear exposition of this crucial DGB position, see Günter Pehl, 'Schafft der Verzicht auf reale Lohnerhöhungen mehr Arbeitsplätze?' *Die Quelle,* February 1978, pp.67–68.

29. See for example: 'Sinkender Dollar lockt deutsche Investoren,' *Die Quelle,* September 1978, p. 484; for good data see Pehl, 'Selbständige vergrösserten auch 1977 ihren Einkommensvorsprung,' *Die Quelle,* September 1978, pp. 479–481; and 'Steigende Gewinne und keine neuen Arbeitsplätze,' *Die Quelle,* December 1976, pp. 495–497.

30. See *DGB Report,* No. 11–1, 1978, p. 9.

31. See *DGB Report,* No. 10–4, 1977, p. 6.

32. Pehl, 'Vollbeschäftigung kommt nur mit mutigem, massivem Staatseinsatz zurück,' *Die Quelle,* May 1978, pp. 266–268.

33. For a representative analysis of this set of problems, see Peter Kalmbach, 'Rationalisierung, neue Technologien und Beschäftigung,' *Gewerkschaftliche Monatschefte,* August 1978, pp. 455–465.

34. *Ibid.*

35. *DGB Report,* No. 13–3, 1978, pp. 5–6.

36. Pehl, 'Eine neue internationale Arbeitsteilung setzt sich durch,' *Die Quelle,* May 1978, p. 276.

37. Karl Buschmann, 'Probleme der internationalen Arbeitsteilung in der Textil- und Bekleidungsindustrie,' *Gewerkschaftliche Monatshefte,* June 1978, pp. 355–367.

38. See Berliner Handels- und Frankfurter Bank, 'Wages Purchasing Power Theory— And Practice,' *Economic Review,* No. 711, March 22, 1978.

39. It is highly significant that the German words (literally translated) for employee and employer are respectively *Arbeitnehmer* (work taker) and *Arbeitgeber* (work giver).

40. Karl Hauenschild, 'Es geht auch um Rohstoffe,' *Gewerkschaftliche Umschau,* No. 6, November-December 1977, p. 21.

41. 'Vetter befürchtet totale Konfrontation,' *Frankfurter Rundschau,* January 22, 1979 p. 1.

42. See his 'The Importance of Workers' Control for Revolutionary Change,' *Monthly Review,* XXIX 10 (March 1978), pp. 37–48.

Varieties of Trade Union Weakness: Organised Labour and Capital Formation in Britain, Federal Germany and Sweden

Colin Crouch*

Within a capitalist economy workers and their representatives stand in an ambiguous relationship to investment.[1] At one level, the conflict between labour and capital is between consumption and investment, virtually all investment being financed out of—or influenced by the level of—profits. But the issue is not really that simple. In economic terms, of course, increased consumption will in certain circumstances create a climate of business confidence favourable to investment. But beyond that, wage and salary earners have a clear interest in increased capital formation that will extend productive capacity and create more jobs.

Workers' interest in investment which generates employment is in practice considerably stronger than that of capital, which does not need to make its investment in sectors which will directly increase employment opportunities within the country concerned. It can, for example, loan money to the property markets or finance the deficits of foreign governments, or increase productive capacity overseas, creating employment for labour somewhere, but not in the economy in which the profits were generated. Even if investments are made in productive sectors in the home country, they need not extend employment but may be for purposes of rationalisation and actually lead to a decline in the number of jobs available. Thus it is labour rather than capital which needs certain kinds of investment, but it is entirely dependent on capital for that investment. It is this imbalance in their relationship which determines the subordination of labour to capital.

But that does not end labour's difficulties. Both classes have problems of internal cohesion but those of labour are more severe. There has recently been considerable discussion of differences of interest between fractions of capital, and the state is sometimes presented as representing the 'general' interests of capital when the specific interests of fractions diverge.[2] However, what is usually meant by the general interests of capital are really those of *national* capital; it is only at the level of the nation that the state can represent any general interests. But units of capital are not committed to

*Senior lecturer in Sociology, London School of Economics and Political Science. I have been greatly helped in work on this paper by discussions with John Hughes (Principal of Ruskin College, Oxford) and Gerhard Leminsky (editor-in-chief of *Gewerkschaftliche Monatshefte*), though neither has seen a draft of it or is in any way responsible for any of the views expressed. I am grateful to the Nuffield Foundation for granting me a temporary research fellowship which enabled me to work on the larger project of which this article is a preliminary product.

the interests of any particular nation state. They can escape national boundaries by moving to wherever in the world capital is profitable; similarly, while it makes sense to talk of a difference between different types of capital (financial, industrial, commercial, etc.), capital can relatively easily be converted into different forms depending on how it can maximise its interests. Capital is therefore able to escape conflicts between the general and the specific.

The limiting case for this process occurs when there is a truly general, that is global, crisis of capitalism; when not nation states but international organisations become the representatives of the general interest, or it goes by default. Something of that kind did occur in the inter-war years and it has threatened to recur during the past decade. However, as we shall see below, capital's mobility has increased and there have remained areas of the world of continuing high profitability. While it is ultimately possible for capital to be caught in a global crisis, which its division into specific interests may make it difficult to resolve and from which few units of capital could hope to escape, there are many intermediate levels of crisis from which escape is entirely possible.

The situation of labour is very different. Labour's mobility is immeasurably more constricted than that of capital, whether one thinks of a change in the type of labour (e.g. skill level) or its geographical, especially international, mobility. Workers are almost totally trapped within a given national confine. There are exceptions at the two extremes. The most highly rewarded professional and entrepreneurial skills participate in an international labour market and are able to escape countries with major problems: the very poor may be driven to emigrate by desperation, though they then become totally dependent and subordinate in the country or region to which they move.

While labour is less able to transcend the general context in which it pursues its specific interests, it is also less well equipped to take general consequences into account when engaging in action. While units of capital act only on expert advice, labour's actions are those of badly informed individuals or groups. (The case of a centralised labour movement is a partial exception to which we shall return.)

In sum, while investment is of vital importance to workers they have, within the market economy, no means of affecting its levels or of ensuring that any investment which does take place will create employment in their own labour market. All that is open to them is to try to increase their own consumption[3] through high wage claims. If this action itself threatens investment levels, there is little they can do about it since they are capable only of pursuing immediate interests while investment is a long-term interest.[4] But they are also unable to escape any national crisis to which their action may lead.

The relationship between worker's desire for consumption and their interest in sustained investment has been considered from a somewhat different perspective by Lancaster, who also concludes that a capitalist economy prevents this interest from being realised. He is interested in the consequences of the fact that workers may either save or consume but are unable to control capital accumulation, while capitalists control the allocation of the output not consumed by workers between investment and their own consumption. This presents the workers with a dilemma:

> Should they forego present consumption by handing over part of total income to the capitalists? If they do not, they will obtain no higher consumption in the future. If they do, they have no guarantee that the capitalists will actually invest sufficient of this income to bring about the desired level of increase.

But there is also a dilemma for the capitalists:

> Should they spend now, or accumulate in order to spend more later? If they spend now, they know what they have available. If they accumulate, they may fail to obtain their expected share of the increased output when they come to spend.

The result is sub-optimal investment and thus in the long term a smaller capital stock than could have been achieved.[5]

Lancaster's approach can accommodate organised labour—provided it is orthodox union action which does not change the segregation of the decision spheres of capital and labour, and which is organised on a relatively decentralised, non-strategic basis without effective influence over nationally determined investment levels. However, his arguments are not limited to the case of organised labour, as we are in this paper; workers may be "handing over part of total income to the capitalists" by saving individually, rather than by conscious wage restraint. Seen in this way, wage restraint itself appears as an extraordinary form of savings, in which the saver's agent (the union) allocates some of his savings (the consumption foregone as a result of wage restraint) to an investment fund (the employing company) which offers neither a fixed rate of return nor a share in the equity but merely the *possibility* of an improved return for labour services rendered by the saver!

This illustrates the scope for departure from the path of optimal investment and also the possible variations introduced once we consider labour which is organised. What if labour's organisations are able to break down the capital/labour division? What if they do acquire strategic capacity and an effective voice in national policy able to affect the level of capital formation? What if the mobility of capital is constrained or given institutional incentives to act in more predictable ways than through the free market? It is the aim of this paper to explore some of these possibilities. The central question is: within what kinds of institutional framework is labour most likely to realise its interest in increased capital formation and employment opportunities?

Figure I sets out the casual chain which links workers' interests (in increased consumption and security of employment) to increased investment; it is not of course claimed that the factors discussed here are the sole causes of any one item in the chain. Labour co-operation (in which is included both wage restraint and willingness to accept changes in work organisation, occupational identity, etc.), by affecting the level of profits, will influence the level of investment. This will in turn determine the level of employment.

However, workers are not primarily interested in the overall level of employment, but in the extent to which any expansion of jobs is likely to benefit *them*. Ideally, from their point of view, the jobs are guaranteed or created in their own plant. However, it will also be of interest to them if they are created in labour markets to which they have access, since this both increases their alternative job opportunities and, by raising the overall demand for labour, should lead to increased wages. This security of local labour markets, which is dependent on the overall level of employment, will in turn affect labour's willingness to co-operate.

Figure I: The labour co-operation/investment chain

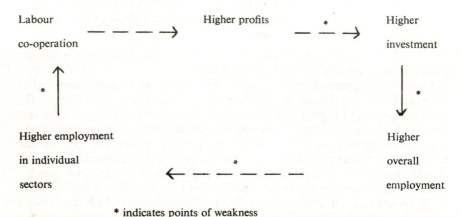

* indicates points of weakness

In a straightforward market economy with organised labour, there will be some slippage in the strength of the relationship at each of the points in the Figure marked with an asterisk. (For present purposes it is assumed that the relationship between union co-operation and increased profits is unproblematic.) Of course, if labour is weakly organised, then capital is less dependent on its co-operation and the importance of this chain to overall investment levels in the economy is less important. However, if labour is strong, any slippage at any point in the chain could, unless checked, lead to a vicious spiral of declining investment, reduced employment, and reduced labour co-operation—until it reaches a point of equilibrium where the loss of jobs in the economy has proceeded so far that labour is weakened and its co-operation no longer matters. Given the mobility of capital and the points established by Lancaster, the opportunities for such slippage in a market economy are considerable.

Additional problems concern the dilemma between consumption and investment faced by unions in their bargaining policy. While investment is, in the conditions established above, in labour's interests, it is a more long-term interest than that in the immediate goals of increased consumption. Economic actors are only able to pursue long-term interests if they have some strategic capacity; that is, if the consequences of their actions have a discernible macro-economic effect.[6] Centralised union movements are therefore more likely to give priority to investment goals than decentralised ones. Given that most movements need to pay some attention to both centralising and decentralising influences, the tension imposed by the dilemma is likely to be felt whatever overall choice is made. For many years the most attractive resolution of the dilemma for unions has been Keynesian economic policy. This (at least in the versions preferred by unions) stresses the stimulation that can be given to investment by demand, assisted by public spending. This suits union interests in that it both reconciles consumption and investment interests *and*, by stressing public spending, removes some discretion and mobility from capital in determining the pace of economic development. Further, the commitment to full employment of Keynesian economics helps ensure that increased investment will be accompanied by the creation and protection of jobs. These policies therefore act directly on two of the four points of potential slippage in the investment chain. They may also contribute to labour co-operation in that they give unions and workers confidence that full employment will be guaranteed in the future.

However, Keynesian policies incorporate two weaknesses. First, they operate at the general macro-level of the economy and are unable to guarantee employment opportunities within particular labour markets, or to ease the transition between markets. Second, while facilitating union confidence in job security, they might at certain moments make union co-operation less necessary for the unions, in that governments may be relied on to maintain full employment and public investment whatever happens to labour costs. These lacunae suggest that Keynesian policies alone will be inadequate to sustain a high investment/labour co-operation spiral. In practice, in several countries during the Keynesian era, additional support was provided by the unprecedented economic expansion as western economies took up the slack and the potential for technological development which were the economic legacies of the Second World War.

What policies do unions pursue if simple Keynesianism is not available? This is a question which has confronted western labour movements since the early 1970s, and which is discussed in this paper. We shall do so by looking at the recent record of union economic policy in three countries: Britain, the Federal Republic of Germany and Sweden. However, it is first necessary to examine developments in each of them during the preceding post-war period. We shall do this by looking briefly at the situation relating to the points of potential slippage identified in Figure I.

THE POST-WAR CONTEXT

While Britain is often presented as the principal example of Keynesian economics, this must be seen against the fact that throughout the post-war period the country has also been outstandingly lacking in forces likely to encourage or direct capital into home industrial investment. There have been few institutions encouraging investors to place any priority on industry and a concomitant high level of overseas activity.[7] This can be explained in terms of the legacy of Britain's imperial role and early industrialisation. The latter made it unnecessary for nineteenth century governments to devise particular institutions for channelling credit into productive industry as part of a conscious national strategy of industrialisation; and this, together with the imperial role, made possible the existence of a highly developed and internationally oriented financial sector (the City of London) which had few connections with industry but provided easy and efficient channels for profitable investment elsewhere. At the same time, the importance of the financial institutions to the maintenance of the rate of exchange led the Treasury to place exceptional priority on the needs of this sector, at the expense of those of industrial capital. This was seen most clearly in the near-universal acceptance of a high international value for sterling, even if this led to both an over-pricing of British exports and frequent bouts of deflation carried out to defend the sterling parity, against the commitments of Keynesian policy. Further, as Blank has shown, this also vitiated the effectiveness of the elaborate tripartite apparatus established by British governments to involve unions in economic planning—in order *inter alia* to persuade them to put more confidence in the investment/co-operation chain.[8]

There was therefore considerable slippage in the relationship between profits and investment. The overall level of employment was maintained with greater though inconsistent success. However, in many cases this was achieved by unions being sufficiently strong in the plant to resist improvements in manning levels and work practices made possible by advanced technology (or indeed to resist the technology itself). This of course weakened capital's incentive to invest. At the same time there were no detailed labour-market policies likely to convince workers that adequate alternative employment would be available if they co-operated in the improvement of labour productivity.

The consequences of all this were an economy in which the profitability of industrial investment became low, while capital had exceptional opportunities for escaping from such investment, either to other home applications or overseas.[9] The typical union reaction to this situation throughout the 1950s and 1960s was to regard these inadequacies as grounds for more government intervention in the economy to reduce capital's freedom of manoeuvre, while themselves exploiting their considerable bargaining strength for short-term gain (a policy to which they were in any case inclined as a result of their considerable and growing decentralisation).

Labour tolerated the country's ominous downward investment spiral because it had achieved considerable control over jobs and money wages and was left alone to do so. Capital tolerated it because it had ready means of escape. Meanwhile, the velocity of the spiral was mitigated by the residue of the country's former dominance and the general upward trend of western economies until the exceptional crisis of the 1970s left it dangerously exposed.

The German case offers a complex contrast. Industrial investment has been high and strongly based on export growth. Domestic consumption usually lagged behind overseas trade, starting in the 1940s, when currency reforms and other changes put greatly increased resources at the disposal of capital owners while the mass of the population was still very poor in the wake of the military defeat and consequent social dislocation. Organised labour was weak following years of Nazi persecution and was weakened still further by the waves of displaced persons and refugees entering the country from the east. There were therefore good market reasons to expect a high rate of industrial investment which would not be very dependent on labour co-operation. The strength of future German investment was ensured by a further factor: the existence of institutions likely to facilitate that investment.[10] Following a Bismarckian tradition of state encouragement for industrial development, the Federal Government established the *Kreditanstalt für Wiederaufbau* which made cheap loans available for industrial investment; a separate fund channelled Germany's share of Marshall Aid in the same way (Britain's Marshall Aid was used to repay international loans and was therefore expended through the usual City channels); banks continued their traditionally close relationship with the firms to which they made advances, making possible more long-term guarantees of credit for companies, particularly small ones, than the British banks' traditional short-term loans and overdrafts. The German capital market was poorly developed; there were fewer opportunities for overseas activity, and there was no need to keep the Deutschmark at a high value to meet the interests of finance capital. (In fact, it was deliberately under-valued throughout the 1950s and 1960s.) Lacking a colonial base and, initially, a strong domestic market, German industry was able to secure a commanding position in the crucial markets of the developed world, particularly in capital goods industries.

There was however no pursuit of Keynesian policies as such; the social-market ideology of the Christian Democratic government and orthodox economic opinion prevented it. However, there was a consistent expansionary bias to industry in government credit policy. As a major exporter, Germany benefited from the general climate of international Keynesianism, which kept overseas demand buoyant. Not only did profits lead to a high level of industrial investment with little slippage; until the late 1960s it was investment which generated employment. From the very high levels of the immediate post-war years, unemployment fell to 0.8 per cent by 1960, and, with the slight exceptions of the recession years 1967 and 1968, oscillated between that figure and 0.3 per cent until the international recession of 1974.[11] The protection of labour in particular labour markets took a distinctive and rather corporatist form. Large German firms tried to provide security of employment for the core labour force *(Stammbelegschaft)* of skilled workers, providing career progressions through in-house training schemes and protecting them from shifts in the demand for labour[12]. A large margin of disposable labour *(Randbelegschaft)* was provided by the less skilled, predominantly young, female and immigrant workers. This effectively integrated those sections of the work force most in a position to take organised defensive action if their interests were neglected. The *Betriebsräte* or works councils, the plant level of labour representation which had certain legal powers over personnel questions, consisted overwhelmingly of skilled, male German workers. The unions, whose role in the plant was heavily dependent on their relations with the *Betriebsräte,* officially objected to the discrimination, but union membership was also concentrated among the *Stammbelegschaft,* so there was no real substance in the opposition.

In general organised German labour had good grounds for trusting that co-operation would lead to high investment in the productive sectors; that the level of employment would increase with expanded capacity, and that whatever changes occurred in work practices, the employment and status of skilled groups would be safeguarded. Within the concerns governed by the co-determination laws, workers representatives supported ambitious plans for increased investment put forward by management (sometimes against the representatives of capital).[13]

The relationship between investment and wage restraint was further supported by the centralised structure of the union movement. This made unions likely to take the macro-economic effects of their demands into account during collective bargaining, while at plant level the *Betriebsräte* collaborated with the employers in policies favourable to the skilled work force, leaving little scope for the development of an autonomous, militant shop-floor movement.[14]

If the unions had any complaints it was not that insufficient profits were being channelled back into German industry, but that investment (and therefore profit) was too high in relation to domestic consumption.[15] The unions argued that the heavy dependence on export markets made the economy vulnerable to market fluctuations in other countries and liable to import inflation; the adoption of proper Keynesian policies would enable domestic markets to expand and provide a more stable home base and higher wages.

A shift to a slightly more relaxed stance which incorporated elements of Keynesianism had in fact been developing within German economic opinion since the early 1960s, and it came to fruition in the wake of the 1966–67 recession (the first in a western country since the Second World War).[16] This coincided with the entry to office of the Social Democratic Party, initially as junior partner in the Great Coalition. In particular the SPD Federal Economics Minister, Karl Schiller, was a leading Keynesian. Among the results of this important episode were the establishment of *Konzertierte Aktion* (concerted action), the adoption of certain Keynesian policies to enable the government to stimulate domestic consumption, and in 1969 the revaluation of the Deutschmark. These changes adjusted the balance of German economic development, acknowledging the needs of consumption and the enhanced role of organised labour. Underlying both these changes and the recession which produced them was the fact that the post-war boom was beginning to peter out; it was an early warning of the troubles of the 1970s, for which the Schiller formula has in fact proved inadequate.

The Swedish pattern has been different again. Like Germany, Sweden lacked the English tradition of a highly developed financial sector and possessed an advanced system of government encouragement to investment. But like Britain it did have a powerful labour movement, though one which was highly centralised. It also had an even stronger Keynesian base than

Britain, having adopted Keynesian policies in the 1930s.[17] The Swedes were also keenly aware that their small country was highly dependent on imports while lacking in any natural overseas market. It was therefore a central priority to develop a concerted export and investment strategy; in contrast with Germany it was one in which organised labour was an active participant.

From here developed the series of distinctive Swedish policies which were at least in part made possible by wage restraint and general labour co-operation. As we have noted, straightforward Keynesian policies leave lacunae at the points of employment assurances in specific labour markets and in the incentives to labour to co-operate. After several years of orthodox Keynesianism, Sweden adopted policies which not only tackled the problems arising from these lacunae but also confronted at once all four possible points of slippage identified in Figure I. The central feature was 'solidaristic wage policy'.[18] The unions accepted the central determination of increases in wages, aimed at something between what the most and the least efficient firms could afford to pay. The intended effect of this was to squeeze the less profitable so that they either improved productivity or went out of business. At the same time surplus profits would accumulate in the efficient firms, enabling them to increase investment and expand capacity. The transfer of labour from the less to the more profitable sectors was not left to the market but was assisted by the government through a range of active manpower policies which eased the transition for the workers concerned. Union co-operation in wage restraint and manpower changes directly aided efficiency, making investment in industry attractive to capital and leading to an increase in employment which was additionally guaranteed and encouraged to specific sectors by the state. The government also adopted further interventionist policies, such as the investment reserve fund, which ensured a stable flow of funds to sectors important to national economic strategy.[19] Such a combination of policies made possible further co-operation by the unions to generate a virtuous spiral of investment and labour co-operation.

The system did not operate without problems, in particular those of wage drift, but it did provide a unique combination of union strength and high and profitable investment alongside state intervention in a market economy. There is room for debate over what made such a fruitful combination possible. Several observers stress the longevity of Social Democratic government and the presence of a powerful but centralised union movement. At the same time, Sweden came to occupy a favourable place within capitalist world markets and it is possible to see Swedish labour as a national *Stammbelegschaft* within the European division of labour, protected by a kind of national-level *Betriebsrat* formed by the highly consensual system of national bargaining. Against this, it may be argued that the very fact that the arrangement was worked out at national level enabled it to embrace a wider range of social policy than any individual company deal, with labour able to deploy political as well as industrial strength.

By the end of the 1960s some tensions had appeared in the Swedish system, in particular those associated with the restlessness of skilled labour in profitable companies under solidaristic wages policy. But by the 1970s the situation was also changing in other countries.

DEVELOPMENTS IN THE 1970s

In the past decade there have been major policy shifts in all three countries, and in each case the underlying context has become less favourable to the investment/co-operation chain. The post-war burst of technological innovation leading to rapid economic growth seems to have been exhausted. In many sectors, natural resource constraints have added a further check. The next stages of technological progress seem likely to pose a major threat to employment opportunities rather than an extension of them. At the same time, a range of third-world nations with vast reserves of under-employed labour and poorly developed civil and labour freedoms is beginning to compete with existing industrial countries, both in selling goods and in attracting investment. These developments follow a period in which workers in the industrial countries have been becoming more militant in improving both their incomes and their conditions of work, making them less attractive to capital.

All these factors impose a new tension at every point in the investment chain. Investment is more likely to be leaving the advanced countries for the new "super-competitors",[20] or for sectors of economic activity less affected by commodity crisis, labour problems and erratic trade cycles; what investment does take place is less likely to produce jobs; new job creation is unlikely to be of use to the workers being displaced; and the new shop-floor militancy makes it less easy for union leaderships to participate in an exchange between investment and labour co-operation. Against this background the various union movements have pursued policies designed to reduce the slippage from the spiral, but with indifferent success affected by their existing characteristic weaknesses.

On the general problem of investment in home industry, British and German unions have pursued similar strategies but with obvious differences reflecting the conditions of their economies. The main thrust of their attempts has been consistent with our argument: to reduce the autonomy and mobility of capital, in particular to subordinate it to tripartite control, in order to prevent slippage and make more certain the rewards for wage restraint. The UK has deep structural and sectoral problems with a constantly declining manufacturing sector and a very high marginal propensity to import.[21] The rate of decline has alarmed the Trades Union Congress which, since about 1976, has accepted that there could be no simple solution through general expansion with some government intervention. Most important has been its acceptance that there were constraints on constant credit expansion and that there was little point in a consumption-led boom. It also asserted that there were limits to what could be achieved through global measures or the public ownership of industry.

It now looked far more to *selective* intervention in specific sectors, even in individual firms, and to changes in means for financing industry. As a first step towards this increased selectivity, the TUC strongly backed the policy of the National Economic Development Council of establishing sector working parties (SWPs) in 40 key areas of manufacturing. These were tripartite bodies whose task was to work out an agenda of action to improve industry's export performance and reduce import penetration. The TUC has stood by this policy, though with increasing frustration. The SWPs have been representative mainly of trade associations; the individual unions have found it difficult to develop policies of the technical kind required; and most SWPs have set fairly unambitious targets for expansion rather than accept that they are part of any national plan for achieving more ambitious growth paths.[22]

The unions had seen the SWPs as part of a policy which would include planning agreements. These would be arrangements whereby firms would pursue certain output targets, in exchange for favourable treatment by government. The planning agreement would be governed by a tripartite body, so an element of industrial democracy would enter the system too. The idea was incorporated in the Industry Act 1975, but the Confederation of British Industry was strongly opposed and discouraged firms from co-operating. The TUC therefore became increasingly disappointed and unsuccessfully demanded from the Labour Government an element of compulsion in establishing planning agreements with major companies.

The TUC has had more success in advocating policies of selective investment incentives. These have gradually developed under both Conservative and Labour governments in Britain and provide a range of regionally and industrially based inducements to industry. This selective aid has been financed from general taxation, so its effect has been to reduce the dependence of the economy on the autonomous decisions of capital. It has been the policy of the unions to make this aid increasingly selective, while industrial interests have of course favoured the most general forms of subsidy which leaves decision-making in their hands. For example, most industrial and financial interests have favoured the current indiscriminate 100 per cent depreciation tax allowance on the first year of a new capital investment; the TUC has advocated its replacement by an investment reserve fund on the Swedish model.[23]

The impact of schemes of the kind which have been introduced is limited; particularly when the main thrust of monetary policy has been operating in a contrary direction, constricting the economy. Further, such schemes are only inducements. The unions have therefore demanded other measures for wresting control from private capital and putting it in the hands of public agencies. They supported the establishment of the National Enterprise Board and have advocated strengthening its role. More controversially, they have criticised the operations of the financial sector. In evidence to the Wilson Committee on Financial Services, the TUC advocated establishment of a tripartite body to which a proportion of the funds of insurance companies and pension funds would be allocated.[24] This body would then channel resources to industry in line with national industrial strategy. Similar proposals were made by the unions in the debate over the use of North Sea oil revenue; the TUC wanted the revenues channelled directly into industry, and not to be allowed to slip into the financial markets and away from

British industry. The TUC has also proposed further controls on the export
of capital and the regulation of multi-national companies (major sources of
capital's mobility).[25]

On all these more radical points, the opposition from capital has been
strong and successful. In the debates before the Wilson Committee and
over North Sea oil, the representatives of capital argued that nothing
should be done to prevent capital moving to wherever it is currently most
profitable; earnings from overseas applications would eventually flow back
to Britain, and if British industry could make itself efficient without special
assistance then it might become attractive to investment again.[26] Incentives
should be general (e.g. reduction of direct taxation) rather than specific,
leaving it to the beneficiaries to decide how to allocate their resources.

Some individual firms or even sectors with special problems of import
penetration or lumpy investment cycles have been more attracted to selective
policy, but the general representatives of capital (in particular the CBI)
have minimised the expression of any such views. There has been no overall
admission of any conflict of interest between industrial and financial
capital. All kinds of capital share an interest in keeping government out.
In the British economy, where labour is politically powerful but the City
virtually immune from its influence, all capital is concerned to preserve the
latter as a means of escape from those sectors where labour and the government have managed to constrain capital's autonomy. Further, as pointed
out at the outset, capital's different fractions are prevented from developing
highly distinct interests by the mobility of capital.

Much of what has been said is also relevant to union attempts to ensure
that investment which does take place creates jobs. Several of the investment
incentive schemes are dependent on employment creation. Again, the
unions have had some success with the introduction of various minor
job-protection and job-creation schemes, but little with more radical
policies.

For several years the TUC believed that a return to economic growth
would bring full employment in its train; but more recently it has had grave
doubts. First, it feared that the economy's high propensity to import would
weaken any employment opportunities presented by increased consumption
and constrain the pursuit of expansionary policies. Gradually the TUC
came round to a policy of temporary and selective import penetration
ceilings, backed by sectoral policies (including planning agreements) to
ensure that the advantages presented by protection were not wasted.[27]

The unions also became interested in the new industrial competitors in
the Third World; in particular they were concerned that labour in these
countries was cheap and weak, giving capital the opportunity to price
western goods out of world markets and bring enormous pressure to bear
on the position labour had achieved in the advanced industrial countries.
The TUC therefore advocated both domestic action and international
measures through reform of the General Agreement on Tariffs and Trade
to permit discrimination against countries with poor labour standards.
But it was not until 1979 that the TUC took seriously the major long-term
threat to employment in the UK economy: the new technology or micro-

processors.[28] Even then, being strongly committed to a policy of expansion through new investment, it did not take the view that these developments should be resisted. Its concern was with offsetting and mitigating the employment effects through proper planning of the adjustment and through expansion of public sector employment in areas which would be unaffected.

TUC policies have entirely lacked measures of the Swedish kind for linking labour market changes to wages policy. This brings us to a central weakness in its whole attempt to influence investment policy. The unions are making demands hostile to the interests of capital, but with little capacity either to *mobilise* their own members in support of the demands or to *offer* effective co-operation as the price of concessions from capital and the state. From 1975–78 they did give considerable general support to wage restraint, and in part it was this that gave them leverage over the various investment and job-protection policies that were adopted. But there is no evidence that the unions could mobilise members for action on investment policy other than purely defensive measures to save employment in individual unprofitable plants, which may often have the consequence of deflecting resources from the industrial strategy rather than contributing to it. At the heart of this are both the decentralised nature of the union movement and the inability of the country to develop a policy of expansion which could have given confidence to workers in threatened sectors that alternative job chances would be available.

The TUC was in principle aware of the need for national policies to be ratified in measures lower down; it spoke of four levels of the economy: national, sectoral, company and plant.[29] But there was little success in giving practical effect to this vision. The TUC regularly exhorted company and plant-level union representatives to press industrial strategy demands as an extension of collective bargaining, and organised conferences to inform them of the strategy. But the records of collective bargaining over the period show little evidence of attempts by bargainers to extend their role in this way, even though the existence of an incomes policy for most of the period left union representatives in need of bargainable issues. At the same time, government and employers refused to concede to company and plant representatives the authority to participate in decisions of that kind. The CBI effectively resisted both planning agreements and the proposals for worker participation at board level made by the majority report of the Bullock Committee.[30] Even the sector working parties established under NEDC did not make possible distinctive union policies, if only because most unions lacked the technical resources to provide a substantial input. Thus, while there were ostensibly many changes in British political economy during the 1970s which gave the unions far stronger formal participation in decision-making, little was really done which would enable them to take part in an exchange of co-operation for investment. Meanwhile, the overall structure of the economy, combined with its past record of failure, continued to reinforce the existing downward spiral.

Many of the problems faced in Britain were absent from the German situation. The external trade balance presented problems of surplus, not deficit, so the entire debate over import penetration was missing. Levels of efficiency were also very high. But there have been difficulties. Under the post-1971 regime of floating exchange rates the Deutschmark has no longer been kept artificially low. One effect of its rising value has been to make German unit labour costs the highest in the world. At the same time, labour has become more militant. German capital has responded by demanding even more wage moderation and by repeatedly pointing to the wage-profit-investment-employment cycle.

Whereas in previous years this relationship might have worked convincingly, it is now ceasing to do so.[31] Unemployment reached 3.8 per cent in the years since 1974, while the extreme aversion to inflation in the German economy has led the government to take very few reflationary risks. Even though private investment has been declining and public investment has been the main source of employment creation, the government has reduced public investment.[32]

Capital formation remains high by British standards but it is increasingly less likely to generate employment, particularly in sectors and regions with structural problems, like textiles and steel. For several years there has been evidence that firms have responded to declining profitability by investing in rationalisation rather than in the extension of capacity, leading to a reduction rather than an expansion of jobs.[33] Of even greater long-term significance are the threats from new technology and from third-world competitors discussed in connection with Britain. The "super-competitors" are seen somewhat differently by the German unions; it is not so much the threat from import penetration as that of a flight of capital from Germany to these new countries which worries them.[34] Germany has fewer controls over capital exports than Britain had until very recently, and its capital has nothing like the long record of overseas activity characteristic of British companies (an important element in its earlier virtuous spiral of investment and labour co-operation).[35]

Meanwhile, it is becoming less easy for German unions to maintain the cohesion of the movement around centralised, co-operative policies. This was first seen in the important strikes in September 1969 and has developed since. One factor has been the declining power of the *Stammbelegschaft* policy. Many groups of marginal workers have begun to organise, while the sectors with big structural problems have had difficulty in protecting even the skilled workers.[36]

In response to this deterioration of the investment/co-operation spiral the unions have responded with policies similar to those advanced in Britain, and with a similarly patchy record of success. Their central demand has been for *Investitionslenkung,* a series of policies whereby the government would steer investment to points where it was needed for an overall growth strategy and in order to stimulate employment.[37] Like the TUC the *Deutsche Gewerkschaftsbund* believes that overall economic management is inadequate for contemporary problems and needs to be supplemented by specific regional and sectoral policies; similarly, subsidies to companies should not be given indiscriminately but consistent with a policy of increasing employment opportunities.[38] However, the German unions would be unlikely to support policies requiring intervention in specific firms along British planning agreement lines.[39] They consider that this would threaten bargaining autonomy and also reduce the role of the company *Aufsichtsräte,* on which workers are represented.

While maintaining a wide range of subsidies to troubled sectors and of job-creation and protection schemes, the government has rejected *Investitionslenkung,* while German capital has been active in preventing any encroachments on its rights. For example, several important employers' associations opposed the extension of *Mitbestimmung* in large companies.

The unions' general demands on investment are therefore closely linked to policies for expanding employment. In addition they have extended orthodox Keynesian demands to meet the challenge to full employment raised by new technology. Alongside high-technology industries manned by properly trained workers, the DGB wants to see a major expansion of public-sector employment in education, the social services, environmental protection and other areas where labour is still needed.[40] At the same time, the stimulus to demand would reduce Germany's export-dependence.

The weakness of British unions in reaching agreements on investment issues has been that their militancy and mobilisation base has been at the shop floor, remote from the point at which strategic decisions are made, and we have seen how attempts by the TUC to diffuse interest in investment policy have met with little success. German unions have been far more centralised, and in addition possess the research capacity which would enable them to participate more effectively in detailed economic policies. However, they have lacked the capacity to mobilise workers behind these centrally determined policies, for a variety of reasons which go to the heart of the weakness of German organised labour.

The *Betriebsräte* have an interest in company-level investment plans, as do workers' representsative on *Aufsichtsräte* in the large companies, but they have been very much tied to the interests of the particular company concerned and are not available for mobilisation behind a national trade-union strategy. At company level it is not possible for workers' representatives to do much more than follow the interests of the particular concern within the prevailing market environment, while union strategy is calling for a change in the parameters of that environment.[41] The unions have tried to tackle this *Betriebsegoismus* through their minority representation within the workers' side of *Aufsichtsräte,* but their scope for doing so is extremely limited, given the preponderance of company interests. There is certainly no possibility for the unions to pursue a national policy of improving employment opportunities through investment by co-ordinating individual *Aufsichtsräte,* setting aside the fact that in most of these the workers are in a minority.[42]

To meet this issue the unions have revived a long-standing demand for *Wirtschafts- und Sozialräte,* tripartite bodies at federal, *Land,* and regional level which would agree an overall economic strategy.[43] When the German unions developed their demand for participation in management under the Weimar Republic, they envisaged company-level participation as merely a part of such a wider edifice. But they have never been able to achieve success at these extra-plant levels, with the result that labour is unable to transcend company interests. While one or two *Länder* have established

Räte there is no sign that the federal government or the employers would be willing to adopt an overall national system. At the same time the unions have not made much progress in developing what they mean by the idea; would such bodies be anything more substantial than NEDC working parties, or the ineffective social and economic councils of France and Italy?

The unions therefore remain unable to wield much influence to relate investment policy to co-operation; their co-operation seems now to be determined by their own weakness, centralisation and continuing rising real incomes. Meanwhile the forces which in the past produced a strong relationship between profits, investment and employment have begun to disintegrate, and with them the German industrial relations consensus. As Markovits and Allen describe elsewhere in this issue, there have recently been major conflicts over issues of new technology and the preservation of employment.

The Swedish case seems to offer the possibility of unions making more headway. As we have seen, the political climate has been more favourable, and the unions have been able to mobilise centrally for policies which linked improvement of the economy to wage restraint *via* employment guarantees with labour mobility. Problems resulted from that policy:[44] restlessness among skilled workers who felt their pay had been held back, and very large profits in the more profitable firms which had been helped by labour's restraint. It is from this inner dynamic of previous policies, rather than from changes in the external environment, that Swedish unions during the 1970s have explored new possibilities of policies linking wage restraint and investment.

In 1976 the *Landesorganisationen* (LO) gave cautious support to proposals for collective capital formation from a working party headed by the economist, Rudolf Meidner. Under these proposals 20 per cent of the profits of Swedish industry would be allocated to employee investment funds administered for each sector of the economy by trade union representatives and a minority of public-interest representatives. Unlike conventional profit-sharing schemes, the shares of the funds would not be distributed to individuals but would be retained, 50 per cent of each year's profits being ploughed back into industry and 50 per cent devoted to collective projects for workers (e.g. trade union education). Given the accumulation of profits the funds would, after a fairly lengthy period, own over half Swedish industry.

Now, the aims of this policy are not primarily related to increasing investment; the authors argue that their effects on capital formation would be neutral.[45] They also acknowledge that for many years they would not act as a major constraint on capital's actions either. The aims of the policy are to complement the solidaristic wage policy, to counteract the concentration of wealth which stems from industrial self-financing and to increase industrial democracy.[46] However, it is clearly a policy which is relevant to the investment problem. It has been the very success of the labour co-operation/high investment/high employment strategy pursued for many years in Sweden which has produced the strains in solidaristic wage policy and failed to reduce the inequality of wealth. The collective capital formation policy is directed to that issue, and may therefore be viewed as a condition for the continuation of the earlier policy.[47] Martin argues that in the long term the profits squeeze on inefficient companies has not been fully offset by excess profits among the efficient, with the result that there has not been enough investment in the more profitable parts to offset reductions in employment in the less profitable parts. The recent prolonged world recession and the high level of Swedish pay settlements in 1974–76 have intensified this trend. The spiral is therefore threatened at every point. There can be no solution acceptable to LO, he says, in generally relaxing the profits squeeze, both on grounds of class distribution and because it would undermine the principle of wage solidarity.[48] The partial collectivisation of profits would avoid these difficulties. In these terms, the policy can therefore be seen as one directly relevant to the investment-co-operation spiral. It is a policy which unambiguously expresses labour's interest in increasing investment and employment under conditions of labour strength in a way that would not be possible for the decentralised, bargaining-preoccupied unions of the UK or for German unions, trapped in a web of co-operation with employers.

The radicalism of the Meidner plan poses a very strong challenge to capital, and there are doubts over the implications of allowing unions such a large stake in ownership of the economy. The Social Democratic Party (SAP) leadership has embraced the policy with great caution, while the bourgeois parties have used it to raise fears of 'totalitarianism'. In the meantime, the loss of office by SAP in 1976 has temporarily stalled any practical progress. At the same time the overall prospects for the Swedish economy are less sound than in the past.[49] Sweden was able to develop its radical Keynesianism against the background of world economic growth. For several years its policies were able to protect the country from the inflation and unemployment which were rising elsewhere. Arrangements for stockpiling production and such schemes as the investment reserve sustained output, so Sweden would have been well placed to take advantage of economic recovery if it had occurred. In the event, the weak recovery of 1976–78 petered out in the face of a new recession. A country of Sweden's size can clearly not affect international developments by its own internal policies. It is therefore heavily dependent on the international economy for its ability to continue to maintain the high level of employment which is a central element in its investment/co-operation chain.

The events of the next few years will indicate whether Swedish labour is capable of holding the unique position it has gained, and of advancing its policy hold on the investment/co-operation chain. Its success or failure will be an important practical test of the potential scope and limitations of organised labour in a capitalist economy. British labour's strength in collective bargaining is exceptional, but it is a strength which feeds on the very liberal economic inheritance which in fact restricts its scope and renders it ultimately self-defeating. The favourable spiral achieved in the Federal German Republic resulted primarily from the passive role of labour within the essentially corporatist legacy of German political economy, in contrast with the activism of the Swedish movement. In order to assert their uncertainly growing strength, the German unions are having to move away from co-operation towards militant bargaining rather than towards anything recognisable as the Swedish model.

NOTES

1. For present purposes we are concerned with capitalist economies, but similar points would apply to a state-owned economy, or any other economic system in which capital is alienated from labour.
2. See, for example, J. Holloway and S. Picciotto (eds.), *State and Capital* (London: Edward Arnold, 1978); and N. Poulantzas, *Political Power and Social Classes* (English edition, London: New Left Books, 1973).
3. Of course, workers may save and invest as well as consume their income, but it would not be possible for them to co-ordinate their actions to produce a rival investment strategy. The same is true of individual profit-sharing schemes organised by many concerns in Germany and a few in Britain. However, different considerations apply when we consider *collective* profit-sharing, as will be discussed in connection with Sweden near the end of the paper.
4. For an extended discussion of 'interests' in labour movements, see C. J. Crouch, "La politique dans les relations industrielles: revendications syndicales et gouvernements dans les années 1970", *Sociologie du Travail*, No. 4, 1979.
5. K. Lancaster, "The Dynamic Inefficiency of Capitalism", *Journal of Political Economy*, Vol. 81, No. 5, 1973, pp. 1095–6; cf. See also E. Jonsson, "Labour as Risk-Bearer", *Cambridge Journal of Economics*, Vol. 2, No. 4, 1978. Lancaster discusses capitalism with the same qualification as in note 1 above.
6. For an account of the importance of labour-movement centralisation applied to the question of inflation, see C. J. Crouch, "The Condition for Trade-Union Wage Restraint: some Lessons from West German and British Experience", in L. N. Lindberg and C. S. Maier (eds.), *The Politics and Sociology of Global Inflation* (Washington D.C.: Brookings Institution, forthcoming); and to the question of economic growth, see M. Olson, "The Political Economy of Comparative Growth Rates" (University of Maryland, mimeo, 1978). I am grateful to Professor Olson for allowing me to see his as yet unpublished paper.
7. Y.-S. Hu, *National Attitudes and the Financing of Industry* (London: PEP, 1975); F. Longsteth, "The City, Industry and the State", in C. J. Crouch (ed.), *State and Economy in Contemporary Capitalism* (London: Croom Helm, 1979); S. Strange, *Sterling and British Policy* (London: Oxford University Press, 1971).
8. S. Blank, "Britain: the Politics of Foreign Economic Policy, the Domestic Economy and the Problem of Pluralist Stagnation", *International Organisation*, 31, 4 (1977).
9. J. Hughes, *Funds for Investment* (London: Fabian Society, 1976); NEDO, *Finance for Investment* (London: HMSO, 1975); contributions by A. D. Morgan, S. Holland, C. J. F. Brown and T. D. Sheriff to F. Blackaby (ed.) *De-Industrialisation* (London: Heinemann and NIESR, 1979).
10. M. Welteke, *Theorie und Praxis der Sozialen Marktwirtschaft* (Frankfurt am Main: Campus Verlag, 1976). See also Hu, *op. cit*; and Finance for Industry Ltd., Evidence to Committee to Review the Functioning of Financial Institutions (Wilson Committee), in *Evidence on the Financing of Industry and Trade*, Volume 4 (London: HMSO, 1978), Appendix 1.
11. Figures calculated on a comparable basis for leading industrial nations by US Department of Labor, Bureau of Labor Statistics, *Monthly Labor Review*, June 1972, January 1974.
12. F. Weltz, "Betriebliche Beschäftigungspolitik und Verhalten der Arbeitskräfte", *Gewerkschaftliche Monatshefte*, January 1976, pp. 9–25.
13. D. Brinkmann-Herz, *Entscheidungsprozesse in der Aufsichtsräten der Montanenindustrie* (Berlin: Duncker und Humblot, 1972), p. 149. It is also worth noting that Germany has developed a range of profit-sharing schemes, which can be the subject of collective bargaining. These are of some importance in German industry, though it would be difficult to assess what contribution they make to workers' attitudes to investment (see

special issue on *Vermögenspolitik* of *Gewerkschaftliche Monatshefte,* February 1972). There have been debates over the possibility of *collective* profit-sharing schemes similar to the Swedish proposal discussed towards the end of this paper, but the issue is of little practical significance.

14. W. Streeck, "Organisational Consequences of Corporatist Co-operation in West German Labour Unions: a Case Study" (Berlin: Internationales Institut für Management und Verwaltung, 1978); and *idem,* "Gewerkschafts-Organisation und Industrielle Beziehungen", (Proceedings of 19. Soziologentag der Deutschen Gesellschaft für Soziologie, forthcoming).

15. H.-D. Hardes, *Einkommenspolitik in der BRD* (Frankfurt am Main: Herder und Herder, 1974).

16. *Ibid;* see also N. Kloten *et al,* "Domestic Factors in the Stabilization Success of the Federal Republic", in Lindberg and Maier (eds.), op. cit.

17. A. Martin, "The Dynamics of Change in a Keynesian Political Economy: the Swedish Case and its Implications", in C. J. Crouch (ed.), *op. cit; idem,* "Is Democratic Control of Capitalist Economies Possible?", in L. Lindberg *et al* (eds.) *Stress and Contradiction in Modern Capitalism* (Lexington: D. C. Heath, 1975); *idem,* "Sweden and the Limits of Investment and Growth", in Lindberg and Meier (eds.) *op. cit.*

18. D. Robinson, *Solidaristic Wage Policy in Sweden* (Paris: OECD, 1974).

19. Under the investment reserve fund schemes, firms set aside some of their profits in blocked accounts with the central bank. These profits are tax-free if the firms only draw on them for investment at times specified by the government. See G. Eliasson, *Investment Funds in Operation* (Stockholm: National Institute of Economic Research, 1965).

20. A term devised by the TUC, *TUC Economic Review 1979* (London; TUC, 1979), para 73, to describe the new industrial third-world countries.

21. A. Singh, "UK Industry and the World Economy: a Case of De-Industrialisation?", *Cambridge Journal of Economies,* June 1977; Blackaby (ed.), op. cit.

22. TUC, *Economic Review 1977,* pp. 36–42. The TUC sets out its main assessment and policy demands in its annual *Trades Union Congress Economic Review,* on which much of the preceding is based.

23. *Ibid,* paras 113, 114.

24. TUC, Evidence to Wilson Committee, *Evidence on the Financing of Industry and Trade,* Volume 2.

25. TUC, *Report of General Council 1978,* p. 293 (London: TUC, 1979); TUC, *Economic Review 1978,* pp. 36, 37; *Economic Review 1979,* para. 87.

26. See the evidence to the Wilson Committee of the CBI and the Association of Independent Businesses (Vol. 2); the Stock Exchange (Vol, 3); Finance for Industry Ltd. and Equity Capital for Industry (Vol. 4); Association of British Chambers of Commerce (Vol. 7.).

27. TUC, *Economic Review 1976,* paras. 99–109; the policy was further elaborated in subsequent years.

28. *Ibid, 1979,* paras. 1–32; cf. 73–84.

29. *Ibid, 1975,* paras. 70–72.

30. J. Elliott, *Conflict or Co-operation? The Growth of Industrial Democracy* (London: Kogan Page, 1978).

31. R. Jordan and H. Kuchle, "Investitionslücke und gewerkschaftliche Schlussfolgerungen", *Gewerkschaftliche Monatshefte,* August 1978, pp. 465–476.

32. OECD, *Economic Survey of Germany* (Paris: OECD, pp. 39–45).

33. Welteke, *op. cit.,* pp. 186–196.

34. E. Loderer, "Strukturelle Arbeitslosigkeit durch technologischen Wandel", *Gewerkschaftliche Monatshefte,* July 1977, pp. 409–417; U. Zachert, "Rationalisierung—Stillegung—Arbeitsplatzverlust: Möglichkeiten und Perspektiven gewerkschaftlicher Gegenwehr", *ibid,* pp. 281–129; P. Kalmbach, "Rationalisierung, neue Technologien und Beschäftigung, *ibid,* 1978, pp. 455–465. F. Fröbel, J. Heinrichs, O. Kreye, *Die Neue Internationale Arbeitsteilung: Strukturelle Arbeitslosigkeit in den Industrieländern und die Industrialisierung der Entwicklungsländer* (Hamberg: Reinbek, 1977).

35. For comparative data on West Germany, the UK, the USA and Japan, see A. D. Morgan, "Foreign Manufacturing by UK Firms", in Blackaby (ed.), *op. cit.*

36. H. Korn and H. Schauer, "Rationalisierungs- und Besitzstandssicherung in der Metallindustrie", Part I, *Gewerkschaftliche Monatshefte,* May 1978, pp. 272–91. But see B. Lutz, "Sieben magere Jahre–oder: Ist die Unterbeschäftigung vermeidlich?", in U. Borsdorf *et al* (eds.) *Gewerkschaftliche Politik: Reform aus Solidarität* (Cologne: Bund Verlag, 1977). See also W. Müller-Jentsch and H.-J. Sperling, "Economic Development, Labour Conflicts and the Industrial Relations System in West Germany", in C. J. Crouch and A. Pizzorno (eds.) *The Resurgence of Class Conflict in Western Europe since 1968,* Volume 1, *National Studies* (London: Macmillan, 1978).

37. *WSI-Mitteilungen,* nos. 10, 11, 12, 1976; H. Markmann, "Strukturwandel und Investitionslenkung", in Borsdorf *et al* (eds.), *op. cit.*

38. DGB, *Vorschläge des DGB zur Wiederherstellung der Vollbeschäftigung* (Dusseldorf: DBG, 1977), pp. 15, 16.

39. Markmann, *op. cit.,* p. 442.

40. DGB, *op. cit.,* pp. 12, 13, 20.

41. T. Kirkwood and H. Mewes, "The Limits of Trade-Unions Power in the Capitalist Order: the Case of West German Labour's Quest for Co-Determination", *British Journal of Industrial Relations,* XIV, 3, pp. 295–305 (1976).

42. The contribution of trade union nominees on *Aufsichtsräte* to combatting *Betriebsegoismus* was recognised by the Biedenkopf Commission on co-determination (*Mitbestimmung im Unternehmen,* Bochum, 1972, ch. III para. 14). However, neither the Commission nor the new *Mitbestimmungsgesetz* of 1976 proposed an increase in the proportion of union nominees within the workers' side. The *Betriebsräte* are in several respects also an aspect of co-determination. The rights and scope of *Betriebsräte* were greatly extended in the *Betriebsverfassungsgesetz,* 1972; and in 1976 a new *Mitbestimmungsgesetz* increased worker membership of *Aufsichtsräte* outside coal and steel to an apparent 50 per cent—but a representative of senior management *(leitende Angestellte)* was included on the *workers' side.*

43. W. Kaltenborn, "Probleme Gesamtwirtschaftlicher Mitbestimmung", *Gewerkschaftliche Monatshefte,* October 1973.

44. C. Van Otter "Sweden: Labor Reformism Reshapes the System", in S. Barkin (ed.), *Worker Militancy and its Consequences 1965–75* (New York: Praeger, 1975).

45. R. Meidner, *Employee Investment Funds* (English edition: London: Allen and Unwin, 1978) pp. 113–119; Martin, in Crouch (ed.), *op. cit.*

46. Meidner, p. 15.

47. *Ibid,* ch. 3. Meidner does also argue that in the long run the funds could be used to ensure that there is no flight of capital from Sweden (p. 61), and that employee-controlled companies would be more sensitive than capitalists to the needs of national industrial and employment policy (p. 79).

48. Martin, in Crouch (ed.), *op. cit.,* pp. 114–117.

49. OCED, *Economic Survey of Sweden,* 1977 and 1978 (Paris: OECD, 1977 and 1978 respectively).

Trade Union Strategies and Social Policy in Italy and Sweden

Marino Regini and Gösta Esping-Andersen*

THE ROLE OF SOCIAL POLICY IN DIFFERENT TRADE UNION STRATEGIES

All trade unions in capitalist countries pursue some combination of two basic objectives. Firstly, they try to enhance their members' economic and working conditions. In the short term, economic interests of employed workers are usually satisfied by achieving both direct or indirect wage increases and job and income security. Besides the obvious purpose of furthering members' interests, such achievements may also serve the organisational need to attract potential members.[1] Secondly, to a greater or lesser extent, all trade unions are also interested in full employment and economic growth. In the long term, wage increases and job and income security can only be ensured by economic growth and by full employment, as this maximises the market power of employed workers. As far as the organisational interests of unions are concerned, full employment swells the number of wage and salary earners, therefore of potential union members.

What role can social policy play through the expansion of the welfare state, in the possibility of achieving these two goals? What place will, therefore, be assigned in trade union strategies to supporting social policy and trying to influence its content? Different types of union movement will be differentially willing and able to utilise potentially positive elements for their strategy.

Trade unions which only represent the interests of their actual members, pursuing them almost exclusively through labour market action, are unlikely to see any substantial advantages in supporting social policy. To be sure, social policies can increase workers' job and income security. But this type of union usually has other ways of attaining such objectives: job control, private pension schemes and wage guarantees bargained with employers, or friendly society activities directly performed by the unions themselves. These means may well be preferred to social security provided by the state at very high cost and for all citizens. Also, social expenditure can cover 'social investment' and 'social consumption',[2] therefore helping capital accumulation necessary to secure full employment, as well as providing social services which indirectly increase real wages. But this use of social expenditure and the desired results are by no means automatic: cap-

*Marino Regini teaches sociology at the University of Milan. Gösta Esping-Andersen teaches sociology at Harvard University.

ital accumulation may be directed to increasing rationalisation and not to labour-intensive investments; social services may benefit other social groups more than workers. Unions acting predominantly through collective bargaining for their members only, usually lack the political power and legitimation needed to ensure that social expenditure be used in their own interests. This type of union is, therefore, neither willing nor able to assign a central role in its strategy towards state social policy.

The picture may, however, change for class-oriented unions, which strive for their objectives at least as much through exchange in the political market as through collective bargaining and their labour market power.[3] This type of union, in fact, pursues two other goals, besides the ones discussed above. Class unions seek not only a greater economic and social equality for the whole working class, but also an equalisation of life conditions and of real wages among the different groups of the active population. Furthermore, as they mainly act in the political market, these unions try to enlarge the scope of public steering of the economy. To strengthen their position, they seek directly to control some institutions central to macro-economic policy.

For class-political unions, supporting social policy should be a key element in their strategy. In fact, social policy is usually aimed at income redistribution, hence at achieving greater equality. The expansion of the welfare state is potentially universalistic. Also, social expenditure has been considered a key way of increasing state management of the economy since Keynes.

As far as the first two objectives of union activity are concerned, class-political unions should be willing to support a public system of social security which covers all workers, over alternative systems of security for the stronger groups in the labour market. Also, they should see some advantages in increasing social expenditure. In fact, as class unions acting in the political market, they should on the one hand be able to ensure that it is used to sustain growth and employment; on the other, they should be particularly sensitive to the possibility of creating jobs in this way, as full employment means not only greater market power for the employed workers but also, by enlarging the size of the working class, more power for the unions in the political market. On balance, class-political unions should therefore be most favourable to the expansion of the welfare state, as it increases collective security and equality of living conditions, while it may foster growth and public control over the economy. They can be expected actively to support it and try to influence it in desired directions.

However, all these objectives can only be pursued at the same time in periods of rapid economic expansion. Whenever stagnation and fiscal crisis make their appearance, the welfare state enters a period of deep crisis. The main target for unions becomes to direct resources to preserve full employment, economic stability and the purchasing power of wages, as well as to get sufficient control over the economy to guarantee these objectives. The obvious trade-off is wage moderation and less demand for redistributive policies. A contradiction among the different unions' objectives becomes apparent.

In fact, security and equality, the two old goals of labour movements and of the welfare state, may make both growth and public steering of the economy more difficult. Increasing job and income security and 'excessive' equality may result in 'rigidities' hindering productivity, growth and effective steering of the economy. On the other hand, security and equality may become mutually contradictory. In a situation of scarce resources, effective security for all citizens is very hard to achieve.

How can class-political unions try to cope with such contradictions? To answer this question, we shall analyse the changing behaviour toward social policy of the Swedish and the Italian trade unions. Although by any indicators both these union movements would be classified among those that are class-oriented and active in the political market, a comparison between them may seem rather odd, because they are considered fundamentally different in other respects. Is it not the case that Swedish unions show a very low propensity to strike, an extremely high rate of unionisation, integrated unionism along political lines, high centralisation of union structure and of collective bargaining, participation in corporatist structures;[4] while the Italian unions are just the opposite on all these indicators?

This traditional picture found in comparative studies of industrial relations is still fairly accurate for Sweden but is rapidly becoming obsolete for Italy. While strike activity is still quite high there, all the other indicators have changed in recent years, making Italian unions much more like the Swedish.[5] Not only, therefore, do the two labour movements have crucial points of strategy in common, but Italian unions are now closer in their organisation and behaviour to the Swedish than they are, say, to the French, to which they were traditionally associated in comparative studies. The wide differences in the economic and political structure of the two countries may, on the other hand, help explain much of the difference which remains in the union movements' action.

Our analysis of the changing behaviour of the Swedish and Italian trade unions, therefore, aims at understanding to what extent and under what conditions class-oriented unions, acting in the political market, can cope with the contradictions arising between their goals and achieve some synthesis among them. It will also show what limits their strategies meet in the current situation.

SWEDEN: CAN A SYNTHESIS AMONG DIFFERENT OBJECTIVES BE ACHIEVED?

The evolution of union strategy

The evolution of the Swedish labour movement, and especially the LO, since the Second World War can be characterised in terms of an ever-present tension between its economic growth and full employment objectives on the one hand, and its commitment to increased equality, solidarity and welfare on the other.

In its pursuit of the two goals of equality and full employment, the Swedish unions have adopted a series of major strategies and methods that follow rather clear historical stages. Initially, during the 1930s, the LO adopted the principle of 'solidaristic wage bargaining' as a means of lowering wage differentials among workers, caused by their location in the labour market. Based on national contract settlements, the LO sought to reach collective agreements which ensured that wage differentials between women and men, between workers in high and low unemployment regions, or between workers in high and low profit industries were narrowed. During the late 1940s it was becoming more and more evident that solidaristic wage bargaining was beginning to conflict with the basic objective of full employment and economic stability.[6] To preserve the solidaristic element of union bargaining and to guarantee continued full employment without incurring inflation and eroded export potential, the LO proposed the famous Rehn-model, named after LO-economist Gösta Rehn.

The Rehn model, or what the Swedes call the 'active labour market policy', marks a second step in postwar Swedish union politics. The LO was to continue its solidaristic bargaining and base the national wage contract— applicable to all workers in all industries—on the amount of wage increase permissible among the stronger, more dynamic and more profitable industries. Rather than hold wages back in the less dynamic sectors to protect jobs, the Rehn model proposed a labour market approach whereby workers, laid off in the weaker sectors, be retrained and moved to the stronger sectors in general, and export industries in particular. The Rehn model aims in an indirect way at restructuring the economy by facilitating the mobility of manpower to the more productive sectors. It also seeks to promote productivity growth via extensive training programmes.

The major vehicle for the implementation of the active labour market policy became the so-called *Arbetsmarknadsstyrelsen* (AMS), a central steering organ composed of employer, LO, TCO, SACO and public representatives. Together, the LO and the TCO command a representational majority at the executive level of the AMS. The functions of this corporatistic institution are primarily to facilitate the geographical and sectoral mobility of labour. With massive funds at its disposal, it was authorised to retrain workers with redundant skills, to provide sheltered employment to those workers who for various reasons were difficult to re-educate, and to aid laid-off workers in finding new employment.

During the mid- to late-1960s, the Rehn model began to show signs of weakening as a vehicle for maintaining strong growth and for promoting more equality. The rate of productivity growth was beginning to decline, the problem of uneven economic development was intensifying, and the LO and the TCO began to realise more clearly that an approach based on steering the mobility of labour was insufficient in the longer run. Consequently, the LO and the TCO demanded that more steering of capital investment take place, and that large amounts of pension fund capital be allocated to a publicly controlled investment bank for this purpose. Despite employer pressure on the social democratic government to release pension fund capital in the free lending market as risk capital, the social democrats adopted the union proposal. The establishment of a state investment bank in 1967–1968—linked to the ever more powerful AMS labour market board—introduced a third stage in postwar union struggles to control the economy. One may argue that since the late 1960s, the unions have shifted more and more towards a strategy of steering the mobility of capital. The activities of the state investment bank and the AMS since the late 1960s have thus been focused more sharply on supplementing the labour mobility approach to structural change with direct intervention in the capital market. At first rather timidly, subsequently more aggressively, the AMS and the investment bank began to make direct investments in vital areas of the economy, or to supply capital to low-growth, high unemployment regions.

The unions' strategy of industrial and economic reorganisation did not prove to be wholly successful, as a number of major problems became manifest around 1970 and thereafter. These problems, again, bring out very clearly the dilemma of pursuing a goal of economic growth and of equality simultaneously. To begin with, Sweden's economic growth rate and her rate of productivity increase was still falling behind the OECD average, and that of her major international competitors, thus threatening Sweden's balance of payments and full employment. Second, from the point of view of equality, the unions' economic strategies were meeting growing attacks from rank and file workers. The attacks centered around two significant consequences of union industrial strategy. One, the extraordinary degree of centralisation in the labour movement and in the decision-making and planning structure of the AMS and other such corporatist organs met with a rising militancy. Wildcat strikes which, ostensibly were about wages, appeared under the surface to be a protest against the absence of local influence on decisions which directly affected communities and rank and file workers. Also, workers were increasingly protesting—either militantly, or passively through high absentee rates—against the effects of rationalisation and the single-minded union pursuit of productivity and growth.

The labour movement's adoption of the struggle for industrial, or workplace democracy since the early 1970s is a clear expression of its perceived need to answer these demands for more equality and participation, and less centralisation and hierarchy.

Despite the labour movement's efforts to pursue an aggressive industrial reorganisation strategy by steering the labour and capital market in the 1960s and 1970s, the prospects of continued economic growth and full employment began to look gloomier during the 1970s. Given slow economic growth and high inflation rates, the system of economic steering and the wage bargaining structure are coming under heavy strain. Growing unemployment rates in a number of areas produce a danger of overloading the AMS and the active labour market approach. By 1973, the AMS had to absorb about 150,000 laid-off workers; the figure in 1979 was substantially higher.

In the context of these overlapping structural problems, the LO has begun to struggle for 'economic democracy' legislation, or legislation on the Meidner Plan for collective wage earner funds.[7] In connection with the policies of workplace democracy, the fight for economic democracy signifies the fourth stage in the unions' strategy of controlling the economy. The Meidner Plan would be a major step in the direction of again bringing the promise of more equality and of full employment in harmony. It calls for an annual transfer of twenty percent of company profits to separate wage earner funds which would be controlled by the workers as a collectivity.

This transfer would take the form of collectively owned employee share-holdings in the firm from which the profit transfer takes place. Over a number of decades, the Meidner report has estimated that the wage earner funds would hold a controlling majority in virtually all Swedish firms. Since the wage earners' shares will be targeted for reinvestment, the plan deals with the problem of continued capital formation and economic growth. Since it entails a gradual redistribution of capital ownership to the employees' collectives, the plan also provides a solution to the problem of wealth concentration and equality. Additionally, as a means of redistributing economic resources *between* industries and sectors of the economy, the plan for economic democracy suggests the establishment of a number of regionally based collective funds. These, controlled by the unions, would be earmarked for investment in economically depressed regions, in 'socially desirable' or ordinarily unprofitable areas, or in industries which suffer from under-capitalisation. Collectively owned wage earner capital would also be invested in workplace improvements, such as safety and health issues and more humane technology.

The Swedish Union Movement's Approach to Social Policy

Social policy as a compensating mechanism. The LO's active labour market policy and its aggressive emphasis on stimulating rapid economic growth accelerated the rate of rationalisation, technological change and urbanisation. With its emphasis on maximum labour mobility, retraining and adaptation to advanced technology, LO's labour market strategy heightened the degree of personal and family insecurity and it led to serious disruptions in community and family life. The problem of laid-off workers in declining industries as the active labour market strategy developed was particularly severe. While the whole strategy can be viewed as an *employment policy,* one of the major issues was how to deal with the unemployment which it caused. From the beginning, the LO has always insisted that it retain full control over unemployment compensation programmes. Compared to many other countries (neighbouring Denmark, for example), the basic unemployment insurance programme in Sweden is mainly financed by union member contributions and, to some degree, by state subsidies.[8] Yet, the massive active labour market policy required special legislative attention as to how to deal with lay-offs and those workers who would be eliminated from the open labour market due to age or their inability to be retrained.[9]

Through legislation the problems stemming from the active labour market policy were absorbed within the AMS's activities. The AMS maintains three major programmes to deal with the employment-unemployment issue. First, it sponsors educational and training programmes for those workers willing and capable of retraining, and it helps transfer these workers to new jobs. During retraining, workers are paid almost the same salary as in previous employment. Second, it helps provide sheltered employment (in the public sector, for example) for those workers who are hard to employ or re-educate; older workers, in particular. Third, the AMS includes a large programme dedicated to the rehabilitation of workers, such as the partially disabled, for certain kinds of sheltered employment. Where, for various reasons, reentry into the labour market is impossible, the workers receive special economic support, or they may be entitled to an early pension. As the process of structural change accelerated during the 1960s, the number of workers included in the AMS' programmes increased, as did the number of workers receiving early pension.

Social policy as a mechanism to bolster union strategy. Aside from the union movement's active role in securing educational programmes to promote employment and labour mobility, the most important area of social policy in which the unions have been particularly active on behalf of their overall labour market goals is housing policy.[10] It became evident that the strategy of structural reform in the economy would encounter the problem of housing shortages as the degree of labour mobility into urban centres increased. With such shortages, moreover, the cost of housing would spiral and thus impose a heavy financial burden on workers. The labour movement therefore called for a programme of building one million new units (Sweden's total population is eight million) within ten years. Since such a massive programme would absorb a large amount of productive investment capital, stimulate speculation and inflation in the housing sector, the unions and the social democrats pressed for more public control over the entire finance and production of housing. By first setting the mortgage interest rate well below market level, the Social Democrats ensured that private financial lending would flee the mortgage market. In its place, pension fund capital and state finance was channeled through the AMS as the major source of housing finance. Especially favourable loans were given to cooperative builders, nonprofit housing associations and local authorities so as to reduce the profit incentive in housing construction and gain more control over the nature, distribution and quality of new housing. Of particular importance was the fact that housing development coincided with overall economic planning. Since the late 1960s, when housing shortages were gradually being eliminated, the emphasis of housing policy began to shift towards the issue of equality. A system of rent allowances has been vastly expanded to ensure that lower income families, pensioners and families with children can get access to high quality housing.

Social policy permitting union strategy free play. The conflict over supplementary pensions during the late 1950s was, from the union movement's point of view, as much a struggle to gain more direct control over the capital market as it was a struggle to give manual workers social security coverage commensurable with that of white collar workers. Until the supplementary pension reform in 1958, the Swedish national pension system followed the principles of the Beveridge plan in Great Britain with a flat-rate universal pension, paid out of taxes. During the 1950s, the debate in Sweden revolved around ways in which the pension system could be reformed so as to adjust pension incomes to rising overall incomes and to inflation. The Social Democratic party advocated a reform whereby workers would receive a supplementary pension, financed mainly by employer contributions so as to avoid a steadily growing fiscal burden for pensions. The Social Democrats proposed an earnings-related scheme to supplement the existing flat-rate national pension so that post-retirement incomes closely approximated pre-retirement earnings. The proposal for pension reform provoked one of the most intense and ideologically polarised parliamentary battles in postwar Swedish politics, due to LO's insistence that the new pension funds be controlled by the unions. The decisive shift occurred when the TCO gave tentative support to the reform—particularly the idea of union controlled pension funds—and the Social Democrats were able to persuade individual members of the Liberal party to vote for their bill.

To the LO, seeking to augment its capacity to steer the process of economic growth, the principle of union controlled pension funds was of critical importance. Predictably, these funds would accumulate enormous amounts of capital and would thereby allow the unions considerable leverage over the capital market. Today, the capital in these funds accounts for almost 50 per cent of all investment capital in Sweden. The significance of pension fund capital for later developments can be gauged from their use in housing finance and (since the late 1960s) as investment capital in industry.

ITALY: TOWARDS THE 'DEMOCRATIC STEERING OF THE ECONOMY'?

Among social policies in Italy, we shall focus on the ones aimed at income and job security: old-age, disability, and 'social' pensions; redundancy payments and related employment policies. These are the most intensely debated social policies now. From 1969 to the early seventies, the unions engaged in a struggle for 'social reforms' (of the housing, health, education and transportation systems). This involved many general strikes and bargaining with government, but produced very few results and was soon tacitly abandoned.

Throughout the post-WWII period, the emphasis of Italian unions has slowly shifted from a semi-universalistic system of social security, stressing high benefit standards and equality, to one oriented to growth and compatible with their goal of control over the economy. As they claim to represent general class interests, the majority of Italian unions accepted universal extensions of coverage and demanded equality of benefits for all workers, rather than degrees of protection related to the variable market power of different worker groups. However, as they want to defend their members' interests as well as to foster economic growth and productive employment, they increasingly are against 'welfarism', that is against extending state support to the unproductive part of the population. Their emphasis is on social legislation for all workers and on economic policies which would enlarge employment, rather than on adequate social security for all citizens.[11] This explains why, for instance, Italian unions never favoured subsidies to the unemployed, but rather wage security for the employed in case of lay-offs, together with industrial restructuring to make firms more efficient; or why they never exerted pressures for substantial welfare allowances, while demanding high old-age pensions and insisting on investments to create new jobs.

As we shall see, partly against their expectations, Italian unions have therefore obtained a rather high level of security for their potential members (wage earners in the primary labour market), but very low levels of protection for others. To fight these inequalities, they do not seek to extend security provisions to the unemployed or to marginal workers, but to reform the existing system so as to make it compatible with economic growth creating productive employment.

The politics of the pension system[12]

In the 1950s and 60s, the pension system developed through pressure politics in two directions: extension of minimum coverage to new groups of non-wage-earner workers and rise in benefits for wage earners. These goals were largely shared by the labour unions, although they did not play an active role in coverage extensions. From 1950 to 1963, different types of old-age and disability pensions were introduced by law for various professional, white collar and self-employed workers, farmers, artisans, housewives, and, finally, shop-keepers. Most of these categories won a right to a minimum pension allowance irrespective of the contributions paid. While the initiative in all these cases came from the government, interested in the electoral consensus of these social groups, the unions were not generally opposed. They demanded that these extensions be financed by the state and not, as it was, by the assets of the industrial pension administration. In other words, they feared interference with the interests of industrial employees and employers, while they were not concerned, at that time, with a possible fiscal crisis of the state.

Actually, the unions never liked this unplanned, piecemeal expansion of a system of 'unequal universalism' but in the '50s and early '60s they were not strong enough to oppose it. They basically confined their action to defending their members' immediate interests, while continuously demanding a reform of the whole pension system. As they became stronger in the political market in the late '60s and in the '70s, however, they tried harder to influence pension policies according to their basic goals.

High income security for their rank and file obviously retained its prominence. In the late '60s, this was reflected in the central demand for earnings-related pensions. After succeeding in relating pensions to the previous income of the retiring worker in the proportion of 80 per cent, in 1975 the unions could tie periodic pension increases to the average wage rises in industry.

Together with this substantial rise in old-age pension benefits, the unions proposed and obtained a state-financed 'social pension' for all citizens over 65, which is actually just a token, means-tested welfare allowance. They also accepted norms on disability pensions which allow them to be used as disguised, though quite low, subsidies to marginal workers. Fairly high benefit standards for the primary labour force were, therefore, achieved together with some (though low) degree of protection for other groups of the population; unions' distaste for 'welfarism' was still partly overcome by lack of concern for the fiscal crisis of the state.

Equality among the groups of workers covered by social insurance had long inspired the many proposals set forth by the unions for a reform of the pension system ever since the war. These unanswered proposals were centred around the equalisation of benefits for all workers (wage earners or not), through a common system partly financed by the state. In 1967, the CGIL strongly opposed the government's reform proposal to create two pension systems: a statutory, state-financed, universalistic one, and a supplementary, collectively bargained system at industry level. This proposal was in fact considered anti-egalitarian, while the unions exerted strong pressure in favour of setting a minimum pension allowance (irrespective of contributions paid) equal for all categories of workers as well as equal pension increases, both based on contractual wages of industrial workers.[13]

Control over basic features of the economy gradually became prominent as an objective to which union demands concerning pensions were oriented. The long-demanded majority participation of union representatives in the board of directors of INPS—the national public agency administering pensions—was finally granted by a 1969 law, which ratified an agreement reached between government and the unions. Control over INPS could potentially provide the unions with great economic power, were they able to use pension funds as an instrument to intervene in the economy, as was done in Sweden. But Italian unions apparently hesitate to use INPS in such a way. This probably has to do both with their past strong criticism of the use made of INPS as an instrument for political power, and with the limitations to their actual control over this agency set by the strict legal controls over the board of directors' activities. Fairly high income security for their members, a limited degree of universalism through low welfare provisions paid for by the state, equality among the workers insured, control over the whole pension system were, therefore, the goals pursued by the unions up to the early seventies. Their very experience as managers of a public agency confronting enormous and growing deficits, however, slowly changed their attitude toward social security. The role of social expenditure in creating inflation and fiscal crisis, in a period of deep economic crisis, alerted the unions to the possible contradiction between security and equality on the one hand and economic growth on the other. To help an effective public steering of the economy and maintain legitimacy as representatives of general interests (now largely identified with full employment and growth), the unions have to try to use their power in a 'responsible' way.

Of course they cannot antagonise their members by decreasing the level of old-age benefits, especially as these are now largely a consequence of automatic increases. But generous granting of disguised welfare provisions, and equalisation of benefits earned by self-employed workers with the higher levels of wage-earners through support by the state, are now seen as incompatible with the new situation. A September 1978 document by CGIL-CISL-UIL, for instance, so defines one of the two basic union objectives for pension reform: "economic-financial balance of pension budgets . . . aimed at equity and at removing waste and privileges". The unions suggest, therefore, cutting state expenditure by reducing the number of disability pensions, by forcing higher contributions from non-wage earners (especially from farmers), whose pensions are a major factor of state deficits, and by increasing controls over payment of contributions due. Growth and control over the economy are now, theoretically, their primary objectives, and social policy is seen more as an obstacle than as an instrument to achieve them. For Italian unions, the welfare state is not a heritage to be harmonised with new needs but something they see as outside their tradition, which aims instead at full employment and at a 'democratic steering of the economy'. But they feel uneasy about suggesting where the welfare state might be cut and their actual behaviour is, therefore, often inconsistent with their stated goals.

From job security to elements of planning?[14]

While unemployment benefits are extremely low in Italy (and the unions never exerted any pressure to get substantial increases), a high level of job security has been achieved mainly through the *Cassa Integrazione Guadagni* (CIG). This is an institution (largely financed by the state) which guarantees a percentage of the salary (93 per cent of net salary in most cases, with almost no time limit) to all workers in industry, construction and agriculture, made partially or totally redundant. Of course, by freezing redundant workers as employees of crisis-ridden firms and guaranteeing their salary, CIG acts as a disincentive to labour mobility.

This institution has been expanded through time though none of the interested parties seemed to like it. Officially, the unions as well as employers and government authorities attack the 'perverse effects' of CIG, but none of them has actually opposed the wider and wider use made of it.[15] The reason is probably that none of the parties would be able to force upon the others solutions more favourable to its own interests (freedom to dismiss for employers vs. an active labour market policy and control over industrial policy for the unions). Actually, Italian labour unions lacked a precise and explicit policy concerning job security until the late sixties. Being weak on the labour market, they by and large accepted whatever institution could somehow defend their members. As late as in 1968, a law largely extending the coverage provided by CIG provided for no active role to be played by the unions. When they became much stronger, they at first (in 1971) tried to win a guaranteed wage through plant-level bargaining in major crisis-ridden firms. In that period, the power of the unions was in fact related to their growing ability to mobilise the workers at the workplace and they tried, therefore, to maximise the immediate interests of their members. They were not concerned with the likely consequences of their own action as yet, this is using their power within a consistent strategy, capable of consolidating their gains. But in 1975 the labour confederation regained the initiative and in a collective agreement with the employers' association, they generalised the results of the earlier plant agreements while trying to make them consistent with their overall objectives. With this agreement, the unions brought CIG's coverage to its maximum; they forced a supplementary 8 per cent contribution from employers willing to use CIG *straordinaria,* to discourage them from asking for state support to meet any difficulty in production; they won a right to be informed and to discuss in advance the actual need to use CIG; and they fostered the government's power either to accept or reject employers' requests for CIG.

The 1975 agreement was the first sign of a turning point in union strategy. On the one hand, by using their new power, the unions still sought and obtained a maximum of income security through egalitarian provisions for their actual and potential members. Besides the improvement of CIG benefits for all redundant workers, with that same agreement they won a maximum egalitarian extension of cost-of-living clauses, and could tie pension increases to the average wage rises in industry. On the other hand, they proved their willingness to adopt a new logic of action: underexploiting their ability to get benefits for their members, in exchange for control over the institutions regulating income security in order to make them compatible with economic growth. Their very success in achieving a fairly high degree of security and equality in 1975 enabled the unions to focus on their other objectives. With the 1975 collective agreement, they sought to discourage employers from solving their problems through lay-offs, and to set the elements of more union and public control over income security. Later on, the labour confederations constantly tried to reduce the role of CIG as a state subsidy to unemployment, while using it selectively, as an instrument of economic policy among others, all oriented to growth.

These other instruments were defined in the following years: a law passed in 1977 under union pressure to facilitate processes of industrial restructuring; various collective agreements at industry level granting the unions rights of information and discussion over investment decisions; a 1978 law to expand youth employment. Many proposals to establish a public agency (similar to the Swedish AMS) under union control to implement an active labour market policy, that is to facilitate labour mobility by hiring laid-off workers, retraining them and finding new job opportunities, have also been debated. The unions have so far opposed such proposals, on the ground that mobility leads to unemployment when the economy is in a recession, and that management of labour supply is ineffective without control over labour demand; but they are likely to compromise soon on creating some institution of this sort. All these laws and agreements are seen by the unions as elements of planning oriented to growth; within this setting they would in exchange moderate their demands for further security and equality, besides practising wage restraint. This new logic of action, however, encounters many limits. A major one has occurred inside the unions themselves. Since the 1975 agreement, a contrast has developed between the labour confederations and a part of the union apparatus on the one hand, aiming at carrying on a consistent economic policy, and some local unions and factory councils on the other, more interested in effectively guaranteeing members' rights.[16] While the labour confederations stress the need for labour mobility (as a prerequisite for growth) and for a selective use of CIG (to make it an instrument of control over entrepreneurial decisions), the factory councils of crisis-ridden firms usually exert pressures for immediate granting of CIG benefits and against mobility. Union action, therefore, is often contradictory: actual behaviour goes in the opposite direction to that required by the stated objectives.

A second major limitation, reinforcing the unions' contradictory behaviour, is the lack of success in the two goals (growth leading to full employment and effective steering of the economy) to which social policy should in their opinion be subordinated. This is due to many factors, to which we shall now turn to try to explain some differences between the Italian and the Swedish unions' behaviour.

COMPARING THE TWO UNION STRATEGIES

Social policy is usually directed at increasing security and equality, but these old objectives of class-oriented labour unions may contradict economic growth and an effective public steering of the economy, which are essential to unions acting in the political market. This leads to an ambivalence of class-political unions toward social policy. Our question was: how can the potential contradiction between the two sets of goals be resolved?

The Italian and the Swedish labour unions have for some time tried to pursue both, with varying success. To summarise, in Sweden the unions have pursued social policy objectives primarily to augment their economic growth strategy. To some degree social policies have merely taken the form of compensation for the negative consequences encountered, and to an extent they have been directly instrumental for LO's growth strategy— housing being a good example. However, in many cases, the formulation of social policy has achieved an impressive synthesis of the two goals. The supplementary pension reform, for example, was designed to both extend pension benefits previously enjoyed only by public sector and white collar workers to LO workers, and it was designed to give the unions more power over the capital market.

In Italy, the unions have for a long time not seen the two sets of goals as contradictory. Being representatives of 'productive' workers they disliked 'welfarist' provisions, but did not oppose them until the state seemed able to support all needs and they had no responsibility in administering social security nor power in the political market. When these conditions changed, the labour confederations tried to show their ability to subordinate security and equality (as well as wages) to growth and opportunity to control the economy. But the trade-off they are seeking does not work; as they are unsuccessful in securing growth and achieving control, a counter-trend not to give up security develops. No synthesis among the different goals seems easily at hand, and their behaviour often looks contradictory.

What are the sources of these differences in the two union movements' attitudes toward social policy and in their ability to give it a positive role in their strategies? Some factors have to do with the different development of social security and with the different history of the labour movements in the two countries. In Sweden, the social security system has been largely a product of the labour movement Social Democratic Party and LO). "By the end of the 1920s the labour movement had become not simply a supporter of social insurance, but positively committed to its aggressive use as a major tool of social policy".[17] Major developments have been initiated and controlled by the unions since then. In Italy, on the other hand, where the

labour movement was weak until the late 1960s, social security was initiated
and expanded in a chaotic way, under the pressure of many sectional
interests to which government responded for clientelistic purposes, with no
overall plans nor concern for internal consistency.

In these conditions, Swedish unions see social security as part of their
own heritage, whose goals must be preserved. But as they have a 'government
culture', they constantly try to harmonise these goals with growth in an
effective way. Italian unions had to confront a system of social security
forged by other forces. As they had an 'opposition culture', they tried to add
their own interests to the ones pursued by others, without seeking any real
synthesis and consistency.[18] This situation has recently changed and so
has the unions' strategy. But they do not have enough power to antagonise
the social groups which would be hit by a rationalisation of social security;
nor enough self-confidence and managerial imagination to use their control
in an aggressive way (for instance, to use pension funds as an active instrument for intervention in the economy as in Sweden); nor enough centralisation
to force their rank and file to accept short-term costs in exchange for long-
term potential benefits. A major example of this difference is the attitude
toward an 'employment agency', which was introduced by the unions
in Sweden while it has so far been opposed by them in Italy. The different
behaviour toward such an institution can largely be explained by the factors
discussed above.

This very example, however, should draw our attention to another
factor, the role played by the economic conditions in the two countries.
Comprehensive reforms of social security and of employment systems are
easier in periods of economic expansion. In the above example, an 'active
labour market policy' supplemented by state aid to laid-off workers (the
Rehn model in Sweden) can be accepted when the prospects for new job
opportunities are favourable. In Italy, the first cases of implementation of
the 1977 law on industrial restructuring show an enormous difficulty for
laid-off workers to be retrained and assisted in finding a new job; actually
they receive CIG subsidies for months, until they leave the labour market.

It is particularly difficult for class unions to harmonise their goal of
equality with security for employed workers, or with guarantees for their
re-employment after being laid-off, when youth unemployment is dramatically
widespread, which it is today in Italy. As an Italian union leader puts it, "a
labour mobility for employed workers, confined within the so-called 'strong'
area of the labour market and isolated . . . from the pressure coming from
young people, from women, from workers in the irregular market, cannot
be accepted by a unitary class movement".[19]

The most important source of the differences, however, is certainly the
relationship of the unions to the party in government. The close association
of LO to the Social Democratic Party in power for decades, not only provided
the Swedish unions with an opportunity to exert a special influence on
social policy, with the consequences indicated earlier. More importantly,
it secured a real willingness and ability on the part of the government to
carry on reforms aimed at equality, growth and control over the economy;
as these goals overlapped with their own, the unions could give something

in exchange and collaborate to make the reforms effective. In Italy, on the contrary, the unions always had to promote reforms aimed at these objectives, against all vested interests represented in the government; while at the same time being reluctant to give up something in exchange. With the government not able or willing to take innovative decisions, the unions must continue to put pressure on it and to bargain over the implementation of a policy even after a law has been passed (as the example of the 1977 law on industrial restructuring shows).

If the differences in the union movements' behaviour can be traced to these factors, some of the constraints they face—as we saw—in pursuing their strategies are largely common. The first limitation is the growing rank-and-file dissatisfaction. In Sweden, it seems particularly directed against the centralisation of union activity needed to pursue such a strategy. In Italy, factory councils and rank-and-file leaders voice their discontent against the sacrifices needed for the trade-off policy pursued by the labour confederations. The second limitation is the degree to which an effective synthesis among the different, potentially contradictory, objectives pursued by the unions through social policy, is dependent on favourable economic and political conditions. These conditions were absent, as we said, in the Italian case, but seem now to be lacking in Sweden as well.

The third limit is the imperfect control held by even powerful unions such as the Swedish and the Italian ones. To secure harmonisation of different goals, unions must be able to control the possible effects of social—as well as of economic—policies. But they lack control over crucial variables, or over decisions which may pre-empt the effects of their control over other variables. An obvious example is inflation. In Italy, a very important example is capital flow to the secondary (irregular) labour market as a consequence of unions' power in the primary one: this has recreated vast inequalities on a larger scale than those eliminated through union action.

All these limitations may make the unions' current strategies toward social policy more difficult. New, more complex paths have probably to be explored. It may well be that, for all the historical differences in the economic and political conditions, the Swedish and the Italian experience will converge in this field. If so, the two labour movements will have to learn from each other how to overcome the crisis of the welfare state and what the slogan 'democratic steering of the economy' may mean concretely in the current situation.

NOTES

1. M. Olson, *The Logic of Collective Action,* Cambridge: Harvard University Press, 1971, p. 39.
2. For these concepts, see J. O'Connor, *The Fiscal Crisis of the State,* New York: St. Martin's Press, 1973.
3. We shall refer to such unions rather imprecisely as 'class—political unions'. The two concepts of 'class union' and of 'political market' have extensively been discussed by Alessandro Pizzorno in two essays. See A. Pizzorno, 'Fra azione di classe e sistemi corporativi', in A. Accornero (ed.), *Problemi del movimento sindacale in Italia 1943–73,* Milano: Feltrinelli, 1976, for the first concept; and A. Pizzorno, 'Political Exchange and Collective Identity in Industrial Conflict', in C. Crouch, A. Pizzorno (eds.),

The Resurgence of Class Conflict in Western Europe Since 1968, vol. 2, London: Macmillan, 1978, for the second one. For our purposes, 'class-oriented unions' are those which systematically try to represent the interests of wider groups than their members alone. Ideally, they represent the interests of what they define as the whole working class. (For instance, they defend the interests of unemployed or marginal workers as well, rather than of regularly employed workers only.) The two characteristics of being class-oriented and of acting mainly in the political market are conceptually distinct, but in practice inter-related. Since it is difficult to pursue the interests of the whole working class (including unemployed and marginal workers) via collective bargaining with employers, class-oriented unions are forced to turn to the state (i.e. to legislation or to bargaining with government) to achieve many of their goals.

4. For the best recent analysis of the Swedish Labour movement, see W. Korpi, *The Working Class in Welfare Capitalism,* London: Routledge & Kegan Paul, 1978. See also A. Martin 'Is Democratic Control of Capitalist Societies Possible?' in L. Lindberg *et al* (eds) *Stress and Contradiction in Modern Capitalism,* Lexington, Mass DC, Heath 1975.

5. The Swedish labour force is the most thoroughly unionised among capitalist countries. LO represents roughly 90 per cent of all manual workers; the TCO organises about 70 per cent of all white collar workers. Finally, SACO which is considerably smaller, represents higher level civil servants, professionals and the like. Except for SACO, which is organised along trade and skill lines, both the LO and the TCO are highly centralised, vertically organised unions based on the principle of industrial unionism. Both the TCO and the LO engage in centralised, national level collective bargaining with the employers' association (SAF). The LO has, since the turn of the century, had intimate ties with the Social Democratic party, but has insisted on maintaining complete autonomy from state intervention in labour market negotiations.

   The Italian Labour force is organised in three labour confederations (plus some minor 'autonomous' unions): the CGIL, which is predominantly communist but includes socialists as well as independents, is the majority confederation (53 per cent of union members in 1977), second largest is the catholic CISL (33.3 per cent); finally, the UIL (13.7 per cent) includes socialists, social democrats and republicans. Since the early seventies, a formal process of unity has been underway, despite great difficulties. The rate of unionisation has steadily increased in this decade and was as high as 59.9 per cent in 1977. (See S. Coi, 'Sindacati in Italia: iscritti, apparato, finanziamento', *Il Mulino* 1979 no. 2. This rate is among the highest in western countries, though somewhat artificially high as it includes unionised pensioners and is computed on notoriously underestimated figures on employment.) Collective bargaining has been largely re-centralised at the national industry level, and union participation in corporatist structures is increasing (see M. Regini, 'Labour Unions, Industrial Action, and Politics', *West European Politics,* 1979, Vol. 2, No. 3 and M. Regini, 'Changing Relationships Between Labour and the State in Italy: Towards a Neo-Corporatist System?', in G. Lehmbruch, P. Schmitter (eds.), *Corporatist Policy Formation in Comparative Perspective,* London: Sage (forthcoming).

6. See R. Meidner, *Samordning och Solidarisk Lönepolitik,* Stockholm: Prisma, 1974; R. Andersson, R. Meidner, *Arbetsmarknadspolitik och Stabilisering,* Stockholm: Prisma, 1973; A. Lindbeck, *Svensk Ekonomisk Politik,* Stockholm: Aldus, 1975.

7. See R. Meidner, *Employee Investment Funds,* London: Allen & Unwin, 1978; E. Asard, *Politik och Ideologi,* Stockholm: Liber Forlag, 1979.

8. H. Heclo, *Modern Social Politics in Britain and Sweden,* New Haven: Yale University Press, 1974.

9. See H. Berglin, A. Lindquist, *Utslagningen paa Arbetsmarknaden,* Lund: Studentliteratur, 1972.

10. See G. Esping-Andersen, 'Social Class, Social Democracy and the State', *Comparative Politics,* 1978, vol. 11, no. 1.

11. An important exception is health insurance. The unions have constantly demanded a national health service for all citizens (of the British type); such a system is in the process of being implemented.

12. Many recent works have analysed the development of the pension system in Italy. See, among others, D. Fausto, *Il sistema italiano di sicurezza sociale,* Bologna: Il Mulino,

1978; O.Castellino, *Il labirinto delle pensioni,* Bologna: Il Mulino, 1976. Very few works, however, deal with the attitudes and the role of labour unions. On this aspect, see the paper given by G. Regonini and M. Graziosi, *Il caso delle pensioni,* at a meeting of the Fondazione Feltrinelli, Milano, March 1979. This is part of a progress report on a larger piece of research coordinated by M. Regini, on which this section largely draws.

13. These demands were part of a more general egalitarian stance of Italian unions, particularly strong in the '60s. During that dacade, wage differentials by sex, age and geographical area, were practically abolished through collective bargaining; also, the differentials among skill levels inside firms were substantially narrowed.

14. This section is largely based on the two following sources: M. Regini, *Politics of Labor Market Policy: Unions and the Labor Market,* paper given at the Conference of Europeanists, Washington, March 1979; I. Regalia, *Appunti sul caso della Cassa Integrazione Guadagni,* paper from a research project report (see note 12 above). A useful work which deals with some of these aspects is: A. Bulgarelli, *Crisi e mobilità operaia,* Milano: Mazzotta, 1978.

15. It has been estimated that in 1975 (the year of deepest crisis and therefore of the largest use of CIG) the number of working hours paid for by CIG was equivalent to the working time of 200,000 people for one year.

16. See I. Regalia, *op. cit.,* p. 26.

17. A. Heidenheimer, H. Heclo, C. Adams, *Comparative Public Policy,* New York: St. Martin's Press, 1975.

18. See G. Amato, *Economia, politica e istituzioni in Italia,* Bologna: Il Mulino, 1976.

19. E. Crea, quoted in *Contrattazione,* 1978 no. 1/2, p. 19.

International Trade Union Collaboration and the Prospects for European Industrial Relations

Emil J. Kirchner*

The establishment of the European Trade Union Confederation (ETUC) in 1973, its expansion since 1974 to include Christian and Communist affiliates, and its dealings with 18 further applicants for membership, raise a number of important questions about trade union representation at national level in Western Europe and for international trade union confederations. Do repercussions of ETUC activity affect either the functions or unity of trade unions in Western European countries? Is the increasing strength and autonomy of the ETUC a threat to the role or existence of the main international trade union confederations? Is the strengthening of the ETUC compatible with the establishment of a large number of independent trade union industry committees at European level? Will the build-up of both types of organisation increase the effectiveness of trade unions to fight multinational enterprises which are substantially non-European in character?

One of the main aims of this paper will be to analyse how the growing membership strength of the ETUC is viewed by international trade union confederations; how the ideological principles of the ETUC converge with or differ from those of international trade union confederations; how the co-operative efforts between the ETUC and European industry trade union committees relate to the aims and objectives of international trade union confederations and industry federations; and how the ETUC and European industry trade union committees respond to European Community (EC) activities, especially in the social field (involving provisions on multinational companies, company law, collective bargaining, etc., and challenges the spheres of action of international trade union confederations and industry federations.

We shall start by identifying the main trade union organisations at international and European level to which confederations of national trade unions and federations of national industry trade unions from Western Europe are affiliated.[1] A further step will be to examine the membership strength and spheres of operation of these different international and European trade union structures and to analyse their relationship to each other. In addition, the extent to which policy concertation or co-operation exists between international and European level trade union structures will be explored, as well as the ways and means of this collaboration. An attempt will also be made to describe the issues on which Western European trade union interests might duplicate, supplement or challenge the activities of international trade union organisations. Finally, the prospects for the emergence of transnational European industrial relations will be considered.

*Lecturer in the Department of Government, University of Essex.

EUROPEAN AND INTERNATIONAL TRADE UNION ORGANISATIONS

Two kinds of trade union organisations at international and European level can be distinguished. Firstly, there are trade union confederations, consisting of the national confederations of trade unions, sometimes referred to as central or umbrella organisations, such as the TUC in Great Britain or the DGB in Germany. Secondly, there are industrial trade unions, consisting of trade unions' members representing workers in specific industries or sectors of the economy, such as metallurgy, chemicals, textiles and agriculture and subsequently we will speak either of international industrial trade union federations, European industrial trade union federations or use the ETUC terminology of European industry committees.

Looking first at trade union confederations at the international level, five central organisations can be identified: International Confederation of Free Trade Unions (ICFTU) with a basically socialist or social democratic outlook; World Confederation of Labour (WCL) which until 1968 used a Christian label but is now not easily categorised; World Federation of Trade Unions (WFTU) denoting a Communist view; International Confederation of Executive Staffs (CIC); International Organisation of National and International Public Service Unions (CIF). The last two are essentially white-collar unions.

Most trade unions in Western Europe, besides their international affiliation to the ICFTU or WCL, are also members of the European level organisation known as the ETUC. Three of the ETUC's members, the Italian CGIL (formerly affiliated to the WFTU), the French CFDT (formerly affiliated to the WCL), and the Irish ICTU, do not belong to any international trade union confederation.

Details of the number of affiliates and the membership strength of the International and European Trade Union Confederations are provided in Table I below.

TABLE 1

EUROPEAN AND INTERNATIONAL TRADE UNIONS AND THEIR MEMBERSHIP (1978)

| | Number of Affiliated Organisations | | Membership Strength | |
	Total	From Western Europe	Total	From Western Europe
CIC	7	7	545,000	545,000
CIF	9	9	1,738,000	1,738,000
ETUC	31	31	40,000,000	40,000,000
ICFTU	122	24	58,645,000	33,500,000
WCL	93	11	15,100,000	2,500,000
WFTU	68	1	180,000,000	2,350,000

Sources: List of affiliated organisations published by the International Confederation of Free Trade Unions, 1 December 1978; Intersocial, no. 49, May 1979, pp. 3–12; Tendances, 8 June 1979, pp. 43–49.

Trade union industrial federations in Western European countries affiliate at international level with one of the following: the 16 International Trade

Secretariats (ITS) related to the ICFTU; the 12 International Trade Federations (ITF) related to the WCL; the 12 Trade Union Internationals (TUI) related to or associated with the WFTU; the six International Branch Federations affiliated to the CIC; the two International Affiliates of the CIF. Of the approximately 16 existing European industrial trade union committees or federations, twelve draw either solely from ITS affiliates or from both the ITS and ITF (and are European counterparts of the ITS and/or ITF), and four recruit solely from the ITF.

RELATIONS BETWEEN INTERNATIONAL TRADE UNION CONFEDERATIONS

Because of the specialised interests, relatively small membership and the European rather than international base of the CIC and CIF, there are almost no links or collaboration between these two organisations and the ICFTU, WFTU and WCL. Relations between the ICFTU and WCL are closer than those which each have individually with the WFTU. However, relations between the WCL and the WFTU are cultivated more than similar ones between the ICFTU and the WFTU. As the main European WCL affiliates are also member organisations of the ETUC, there is a basis for collaboration with ICFTU European members at that level.[2]

Co-operation between the ICFTU and the WCL has taken the form of frequent joint statements defending trade union rights, and of regular joint consultations and actions, particularly in the framework of relations with the International Labour Organisation (ILO) and the Food and Agricultural Organisation of the UN, UNESCO, Economic and Social Council of the UN, as well as other inter-governmental organisations. There is also mutual participation of observers in the two organisations' working groups and occasionally an exchange of observers takes place on other subjects, such as migrant workers. In 1974, the two organisations agreed to establish a joint ICFTU/WCL working committee at executive level, whose aim would be to study the means for developing further co-operation between the two internationals and to seek ways and means for unification.[3] Yet, in spite of having only a quarter of the ICFTU membership, the WCL apparently has very extensive financial resources derived partly from non-member fee contributions, and WCL affiliates fear that these contributions might be lost in a merger with the ICFTU. Another obstacle has been the unwillingness of the two respective regional organisations (ORIT of the ICFTU and CLAT of the WCL) to agree to a merger.[4]

At its nineteenth Congress in 1977, the WCL stated that it was "available for frank and open discussions, as well as for possible communications" with the ICFTU. But at the same Congress, the WCL suggested establishing together with other trade union organisations a centre for contacts, exchanges and co-operation, in order to create conditions favourable to the reorganisation of world trade unionism. Proposals like this slightly irritate the ICFTU as it looks as though the WCL is flirting with the WFTU. Although the CFTU Executive Board set up a Committee on Contrasts with Communist controlled trade union organisations in 1973, it has repeatedly declared that the ICFTU's basic principles did not allow for any relationship with international or regional bodies whose policies were diametrically opposed to free and democratic trade union objectives.

The secretariats of the WCL and WFTU meet jointly twice a year, and each sends delegates to the congress of the other. In addition, the WCL had entered into an anti-ICFTU electoral alliance with the WFTU regarding alleged under-representation in the workers' group of the ILO governing body. Contacts also take place between affiliates of both international organisations, but their value has somewhat diminished since the departure of the French CFDT.[5] The latter has maintained close contacts in France with the CGT, which is an affiliate of the WFTU. The loss of CFDT membership might also undermine WCL potential, if indeed it ever had any, to become a bridge between the ICFTU and the WFTU.

There have been pressures for joint ICFTU/WFTU meetings but except for responding with proposals for closer collaboration in the ILO and with participating in two East-West trade union conferences at the headquarters of the ILO in 1975 and 1977, the ICFTU has taken a tough stand against the WFTU on human rights issues in Eastern Europe since the Helsinki Agreement, which has estranged relations between the two international organisations. Concerning bilateral contacts of its affiliates with WFTU affiliates, the ICFTU has noted that each national centre is free to decide whether or not to engage in such contacts, but if it does, it should inform the ICFTU. Some ICFTU affiliates, like the British TUC, have taken advantage of this opportunity.

Thus, while relations between the ICFTU and WFTU still appear to be troubled, the loss of the French CFDT membership for the WCL and the fact that another of its European mainstays, the Dutch CNV, is urging closer relations with the ICFTU,[6] enhance the prospects for unification between the ICFTU and WCL, which might take place in the medium term.

RELATIONS BETWEEN THE ETUC AND THE ICFTU AND WCL

Of the 31 ETUC affiliates, 22 are also members of the ICFTU and six others are also members of the WCL. The ETUC's founding members were all ICFTU affiliates (in both EC and EFTA countries) and discussions between officials of both the ETUC and the ICFTU in 1973 and 1974 centered on the question of the relationship between the two organisations. Discussions resulted in an agreement between the Executive Committee of the two organisations in 1974, specifying that: the ETUC is an autonomous organisation and not a European regional organisation of the ICFTU and the two organisations operate at two different levels, but form part of the same democratic trade union family.[7] The ETUC was asked to apply the criteria of this agreement in dealing with the then (1974) pending membership applications of WCL affiliates. In the same year, with the Communist trade union of Italy (CGIL) applying for membership, the ETUC once again consulted the ICFTU. When it became clear that the ICFTU Executive Board was unable to give advice, the ETUC Executive Committee decided, in July 1974, by a vote of 21 to 7, in favour of admitting the CGIL.[8]

Whether the admission of the CGIL to the ETUC is an indication, as seen by some affiliates of the ICFTU, of the ETUC adopting a different interpretation of the terms 'democratic' and 'free' from that of the ICFTU, is as yet an open question. The outcome will depend on: the role played by the CGIL, both for the trade union movements in Italy and in the ETUC; and more so, finding satisfactory criteria within the ETUC Executive Committee for the admission of new members, including Communist trade unions from France and Spain.[9]

It appears that a substantial number of members of the ETUC Executive request that CGT, the French communist-led trade union, in line with CGIL entrance conditions, should relinquish its ties with the WFTU and show some flexibility in its anti-EC attitude. So far, the CGT has rejected the 'Italian compromise' and campaigned against direct elections to the European Parliament and condemned the principle of enlarging the EC to incorporate Greece, Spain and Portugal. The same problem might not arise over admission of the Spanish Communist-led trade union, CCOO, which supports Eurocommunism, does not belong to WFTU and favours Spanish accession to the EC.

The most likely supporters of CGT entry to the ETUC—the French CFDT, as well as the British TUC and the Belgian FGTB—will play an important role in the admission; trying to change CGT attitudes and to persuade other Executive members to accept a compromise formula (if there is CGT accommodation) by stressing the importance of regional unity and the anticipated gains in ETUC strength that would result. At stake is not only whether the CGT is admitted, or whether the ICFTU version of 'democracy' can be maintained but also whether certain existing members of the ETUC, predominantly the French CGT-FO, will depart. CGIL membership left some unhealed scars in ETUC cohesion and it is dangerous to aggravate old wounds.[10] There does not seem to be a correlation between renewed consideration for CGT admission to the ETUC and moves for closer co-operation and affiliation between the ETUC and Eastern European trade unions. The latter looks as if it is still only a possibility for the medium to long-term.[11]

If the eighteen applicants are admitted, membership of the ETUC will become increasingly close in size to that of the ICFTU. This might raise the question: will the operation of the ETUC intrude on the competence of either the ICFTU or WCL and/or undermine the existence of both organisations? Asked about these questions, the President of the ETUC replied:

> ... the ETUC is not a substitute for replacing either the policy of the ICFTU or the WCL. The policy of the ICFTU and WCL should not be copied or corrected in the name of the ETUC.... we are not a world organisation. Certainly we have responsibilities with regard to the third world ... [but] it is not a task of the ETUC to establish direct links with the trade unions of the third world. There is no competition between the European and world level. We must be very clear, the goal of the ETUC is not to weaken the ICFTU or WCL, but to support and reinforce them.[12]

Leaving aside the WCL because of its merger prospect with the ICFTU, one can agree at the present time with Windmuller that: "It is vitality rather than sheer survival of the ICFTU which is at stake."[13] In any case, the Secretaries-General of both the ICFTU and WCL have appealed for continued support from the ETUC, which has responded favourably.

Agreements reached between the ETUC and the ICFTU provide that the latter operates largely outside Europe and helps the organisation of trade unions in developing countries, while the former concentrates on activities in Europe and on national organisations dealing particularly with European affairs. The following diagram illustrates which confederations assume consultative status with which international organisations. In practice, this division of labour becomes blurred because the ICFTU and WCL are interested in youth activities and the Social Charter of the OECD, or in the aid and development policy of the EC, while the ETUC has interests in the activities of the ILO.

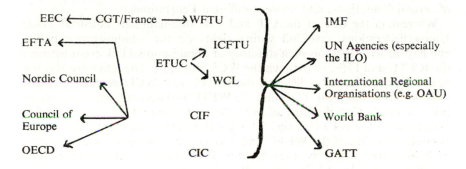

The Secretaries-General of the ICFTU and the ETUC frequently meet to discuss matters of common concern. They also attend, in a consultative capacity, each other's Executive Board or Executive Committee meetings. The Secretary-General of the ETUC also attends the ICFTU/WCL meetings which study ways of developing further co-operation between the two organisations and has frequent contacts with the Secretary-General of the WCL. Furthermore, the ETUC is regularly represented in ICFTU working party meetings. A particularly close working relationship has been established between youth sections of the ICFTU and the ETUC.

Collaboration between the ICFTU and ETUC must also be considered in relation to the possibility of renewed AFL/CIO membership in the ICFTU. While there are presently only signs of a change of heart on the part of the AFL/CIO regarding ICFTU membership, the consequences of such a return are worthwhile considering. The return of the AFL/CIO could balance the lop-sided support presently provided by the European affiliates to the ICFTU and could strengthen the organisation in terms of finance and prestige vis-à-vis the WFTU. On the other hand, AFL/CIO participation might also lessen the interest of the European affiliates in participating vigorously in the ICFTU. Past AFL/CIO support for US involvement in Vietnam might still make some Western European affiliates, notably the

Scandinavians, hesitate to engage in full collaboration with ICFTU policies. Of course, past criticisms by some European affiliates of the ICFTU concerning the AFL/CIO and the dialogue sought by some Western European ICFTU affiliates with trade unions in Eastern Europe, are also factors which the AFL/CIO will weigh up carefully before re-entry. A call for a return of the AFL/CIO might be seen, first as a balancing and strengthening of the ICFTU, second as an alternative to the possibility of losing European resources, managerial skill, leadership and prestige, and third, as a way of improving relations with those International Trade Secretariats (ITS) which view the disaffiliation of the AFL/CIO as a weakening of the whole international free trade union movement.

RELATIONS OF INTERNATIONAL INDUSTRIAL TRADE UNION FEDERATIONS

One can differentiate relations: between certain International Industry Trade Union Federations and Confederations; among individual affiliates of certain federations; and between different Federations.

Whereas in the case of the CIF and CIC International Industrial Trade Union Federations have full voting rights on the administrative bodies and pay subscriptions, no such statutory or organisational link exists between the ICFTU and ITSs, or between the WCL and ITFs. The latter are also not bound by decisions or policies of the ICFTU and WCL, respectively. The relationship between the TUIs and the WFTU is different from the relations just described. Constitutions of individual TUIs might not be in conflict with those of the WFTU. Every TUI has the right to be represented on the controlling bodies of the WFTU and may vote (if voting is done by a show of hands rather than by a card vote). Each TUI can elaborate its own programme within WFTU guidelines. TUIs hold their own conferences with the WFTU secretariat acting as co-ordinator. Each year, TUI secretariats meet the WFTU secretariat to report and co-ordinate. The WFTU also provides part of the TUIs' budgets.[14] While it is the administrative control exercised by the WFTU which impedes the activities and effectiveness of the TUIs, the dismal prospects of the WCL and lack of services causes several individual unions of the ITFs to join the appropriate ITS for their industry, which considerably weakens the vitality of the ITFs.[15]

The relations between the ITS, on the one hand, and the ICFTU, on the other, are governed by an agreement reached in 1951. This agreement of voluntary co-operation gives the ICFTU the right to be represented in an observer capacity at ITS congresses, and lays down the rules of ITS representation: by observers with a consultative voice at ICFTU congresses, meetings of the Executive Board and its committees. In one or two instances, the ICFTU provides financial support for individual ITSs. Thus the ITS have ideological links with the ICFTU but are organisationally independent.[16] Frequency and intensity of contacts vary between individual ITS and the ICFTU. There are indications that the relationship between the ITS and ICFTU has generally become less co-operative. This is not to deny that between some ITSs and the ICFTU a close working relationship exists. Four of five joint ICFTU/ITS strategic meetings on specific questions, as well as on general policy, take place annually. Both have occasionally contributed to the cost of joint programmes for development or solidarity purposes. One of the mainstays in the ICFTU/ITS relations is the joint working party on multinational corporations established in 1972.[17] Relations between unions and multinational corporations at international level fall primarily within the sphere of the ITS, while activities or legislative actions of inter-governmental organisations relating to these corporations primarily concern the ICFTU. Intensity of collaboration among the ITSs varies a great deal. Annually, however, the ITSs organise a general conference among themselves.

RELATIONS OF EUROPEAN INDUSTRIAL TRADE UNION COMMITTEES

At European level a distinction can be made between trade union industrial committees recognised by the ETUC and those with which the ETUC maintains working relations. Acceptance of industry committees is mentioned in Article 4 of the ETUC Constitution and these criteria, as specified by the Executive Committee in 1975, stipulate that an industry committee should have standing bodies, a budget of its own, cover geographically at least the EC countries, and group the concerned trade union industrial federations of the confederation affiliated to the ETUC. In addition, the ETUC and WCL decided in 1974 that in future there would no longer be two European trade union committees for one and the same sector of activity. By the end of 1975, six such industry committees were recognised by the ETUC and with four others working relations existed. In 1979, the respective figures were nine and three.

Certain parallels can be seen in the organisational transformation of European committees into European federations (as with the European Metal Federation) and that experienced by the European trade confederations which started in 1958 as European Secretariats of their international trade union organisations and became autonomous organisations eleven years later. In both instances, respective international ties were and still are of crucial importance to this gradual transformation process. The bone of contention is whether the established organisation is to assist the European regional secretary or conference of the International Federation and to carry out the aims of the International Federation, or whether the organisation is autonomous.

While the EMF and European Federation of Agricultural Workers' Union in the Community (EFA) were most successful in establishing a European identity, for other industrial sectors this is only slowly but gradually developing. Some, like the European Trade Union Committee of Food and Allied Workers in the Community (ETUCF) encountered difficulties in obtaining permission to establish the conditions necessary for ETUC recognition and three have not even obtained that. For the ITS, increased autonomy of the European industrial trade union committee raises not only the question of shared spheres of action but also whether the ITS might get less finance.

All European industrial trade union committees declare in their constitutions that they shall act in close co-operation with their respective international federation and accept only those affiliates which conform to the 'democratic' (some also stipulate the term 'free') principle, and whose national confederations are members of the ETUC. European industrial trade union committees and their respective ITS counterparts collaborate closely on a reciprocal basis, co-ordinate their activity programmes and participate, with a consultative voice, in all the meetings of the administrative bodies. European industry committees also inform their respective ITS of all the important work of the ETUC. Often working groups, such as that on migrant workers, are either administered or have their meetings attended jointly. Studies carried out at one level are passed onto the other level, and sometimes joint investigations are conducted by the ITS and European industrial trade union committees.

Recognised European industry committees are usually represented by their Secretary-General, with a consultative voice at the Executive Committee meetings of the ETUC and with voting rights, except on statutory or financial issues, at the Congress. On the other hand, ETUC representatives are allowed to attend (with a consultative voice) meetings of the governing bodies of the European industry committees. Representatives of the European industry committees participate regularly in the work of the different working groups of the ETUC and are thus able to promote their interests, as well as to contribute to the formulation of ETUC policies. There is also a regular exchange of information, documents and reports between the two Secretariats. Until January 1974, the ETUC administered and financed the secretariat of EFA. A number of European industry committees, especially the EMF, EURO-FIET, ETUCF and EFA, have held joint meetings, exchanged information and, in the case of EFA and ETUCF, developed a joint opinion on the reform of the Community agricultural policy.

Having considered relations and co-operation between different trade union confederations and federations at both international and European level, let us now examine the channels open to and attempts by European trade union organisations to bring about transnational collective bargaining or to influence legislative action concerning multinational firms.

PROSPECTS FOR EUROPEAN INDUSTRIAL RELATIONS

The development of European Community integration in the sixties, promoting multinational corporations with both European and US headquarters, introduced new challenges for trade unions in Western Europe. The threats posed by expanding multinational corporations and the opportunity for involvement in meaningful policy development with such regional organisations as the EC, the Council of Europe, EFTA and the OECD, have all contributed to new transnational organisations and more ambitious trade union goals. One of the major aims of trade unions has been to secure, through collective bargaining agreements at European level, the same rights of information and participation that workers have already in the national context.[18] Another aim is to promote, at European level, the interests which become increasingly difficult to achieve at national level.

Most observers of transnational collective bargaining appear to agree on two characteristics. Firstly, an attenuated form of international collective bargaining will probably develop, on a regional level, within the EC. It will at first, almost certainly, be limited to a particular industry or multinational corporation and, if the latter, most likely one with headquarters in Europe. Secondly, it will not occur in the immediate future.[19] The slow materialisation can largely be attributed to the protracted attitude of multinational corporations and/or employers' organisations towards bargaining at Community level.[20] It is also attributed in part to the inability of the trade unions to narrow sufficiently their national ideological political differences or to balance economic needs with European trade union principles in order to force the issue.[21]

Much of the work that the trade unions have so far done in their attempts to control the activities and operations of multinational firms has been in the nature of preparing the ground for transnational bargaining. Moreover, it is only in the metal working, chemical and food industry sectors, and to some extent in the banking and insurance sectors, that there has been some degree of effective co-ordination and dissemination of information on wages and working conditions, trade union rights, national legislation and labour relations.[22]

The European industrial trade union committees in these sectors carry out similar activities to their international trade secretariats and have set up working groups for the different industry branches at European level. Like the ITS, they have established co-ordination committees on multinational corporations (relating to one company but gathering data in all the European countries in which the company has subsidiaries), such as Philips, Siemens, Volkswagen.[23] The purpose of these worker co-ordination committees is to exchange information and experience and to formulate demands and action plans against multinational firms in regular meetings of delegates from different countries.

European Commission proposals for a European company statute are doubtless of great importance to multinational corporations and trade unions in Western Europe, especially those of EC countries in the future. On the one hand, they will favour mergers of companies located in Europe and thus promote the establishment of multinational corporations. On the other hand, they will represent an attempt to institutionalise worker participation in the management of multinational forms. Part of the draft statute includes provision for a supervisory board, one-third workers' representation on this board, and the establishment of a European works council; while the West German and Dutch unions push especially for this model, other union organisations and the employers are opposed to it.[24] This conflict has so far prevented the European company from becoming a reality.

Similarly, national governments, the EC and OECD have become increasingly involved in studying the value of initiatives and experiments in the field of new work organisation and motivation, such as job enrichment, shop-floor participation in decision-making, asset formation and semi-autonomous work groups which are variably practised in multinational firms like Philips, Olivetti and Volvo. However, trade unions are divided over such schemes in practice, and some would like to prevent them becoming part of a European industrial relations formula. One of the criticisms of these schemes is that they encourage workers' loyalties towards the workplace or company, to the detriment of working class solidarity and also encourage outdated forms of enterprise-oriented labour relations.[25]

While fully fledged regional or Community level collective bargaining agreements might still take some time to come about, an intermediate form of such agreements seems to emerge, containing a limited number of provisions and representing guidelines rather than collectively binding elements. Examples of this can be seen in the two agreements signed between the European Federation of Agricultural Workers' Union in the Community (EFA) ,and the Committee of Professional Agricultural Organisations (COPA) concerning the hours of work per week and number of annual holidays in agriculture. A more recent proposition was made by Wim Kok, president of the ETUC, calling for European agreements in which only the broad outlines of national and sectoral negotiations would be fixed. For example, "one can decide on the principle of a reduction of working time by 10 per cent over four years within the European framework, the choice being left as to its rhythm and styles."[26]

Another attempt to advance industrial relations at Western European level has been made through the use of employment conferences at EC and EFTA level. These conferences are similar to the tripartite structure of the International Labour Organisation (ILO), i.e., workers, employers and government are equally represented. However, while the first relate primarily to employment questions, and their decisions, at least so far, are not binding, the second deal with matters of economic and social policy and can adopt labour standards which give rise to legally binding commitments, as well as their supervision.[27] Although one of the EC employment conferences worked out guidelines on European economic and social policies and was heralded as the first collective Community agreement between the two sides of industry and the EC member governments, they have come under a great deal of criticism, mainly from trade unions but also from the ILO.[28]

In a letter to the European Commission, dated 28 February 1979, the ETUC stated that its Executive Committee would not consider taking part in any further tripartite conference until a number of conditions had been fulfilled, involving the preparation, conduct and duration of such conferences. Alternatively, the ETUC wants to take tougher and more drastic action, including strikes, than that adopted on 5 April 1978. In support of its claims relating to employment, and in view of the exceptional social situation, the ETUC organised a European action day on 5 April 1978. This was the first time that they had promoted action of such wide scope at European level. By work stoppages, demonstrations, assemblies and special meetings in eighteen European countries, workers demonstrated their anxiety and determination in the face of the grave unemployment situation. This tougher approach is in line with Wim Kok's observation that the ETUC is still too often a "paper tiger" in the eyes of the workers: it must become a "tiger with sharp teeth which can bite if necessary."[29]

The strengthening of the ETUC raises questions about its links with national member confederations and its relations with international trade union confederations. The former question involves the issue of whether a closer link is developing between national and European policy and whether there has been a gradual transfer of functions from the national to the European level. Although the acceptance of the recent ETUC action programme by affiliates with priorities on employment and work reduction can be seen as a means whereby national trade unions give powers to their supranational organisation, its limits are evident from the fact that acceptance is not necessarily concurrent with compliance. So far, the ETUC has not matched its growing organisational cohesion with consistent approaches to policies. National ideological differences and accommodating EC interests with EFTA interests, to name some of the main obstacles, make it difficult for the ETUC to take more effective action. The prospect of adding more than a dozen new members to the ETUC will not make that task easier.

Moreover the lack of progress at Community level in social policy harmonisation, especially on social security systems, together with the effects of the economic crisis, perpetuate national orientations of ETUC affiliates and stifle the European orientation of their members.[30] As a consequence, one can agree with Windmuller that: 'It is not likely that the affiliates of the ETUC will, in the near future, turn over any greater portion of their national autonomy to their regional body than they have up until now been willing to cede to their global organisation.'[31]

The existence of the ETUC has affected the ICFTU's authority but so far no serious ideological differences or controversies over policy between the two have shown up. Even closer ties have been maintained between existing European industrial trade union committees/federations and their respective International Trade Secretariats (ITS). Nonetheless, these ties will be stretched the more ETUC and European industry committees develop co-operation.[32] The growing international dimension of the EC in trade, aid and development, especially the application of the Lomé Convention, might make a division of labour between the ETUC and European industry committees, on the one hand, and the ICFTU and ITS, on the other, more difficult.

Perhaps the ETUC will be more successful in obtaining EC legislation concerning the control of multinational corporations than the ICFTU was with the ILO, and the European industrial trade union committees might reach collective bargaining agreements before the ITS. But neither is using a different approach from its international counterpart. Still, there is no guarantee that a European formula for controlling multinational corporations might be effective without being extended to the international plane. Both the ETUC and the European industrial trade union committees must be concerned that if they rush too hard for such controls, without corresponding international development, there is a danger that multinational corporations might leave Western Europe to produce elsewhere and put on the market what has either been produced in developing countries or in Eastern Europe.[33] However, if a start could be made in the European context, to introduce and enforce some code of conduct to which multi-national corporations will be obliged to conform, it might open the way for the adoption of similar international provisions through the ILO or other inter-governmental organisations. The policy of communist countries on Western multinational corporations and the ICFTU willingness to engage in closer co-operation with the WFTU will be of crucial importance in this respect.

Yet while there is an obvious trend towards centralisation in Western Europe, there is already a development within the ETUC which appears to duplicate the dilemma facing the ICFTU and the ETUC. In two cases, inter-regional trade union councils have been established whose task it is to protect and promote the economic, social and cultural interests of workers in their regions.[34] In addition, trade unions in Italy increasingly stress the need for joint action with Mediterranean trade unions. Developments of this kind might undermine ETUC authority but, on the other hand, could contribute to a better understanding of transnational trade union problems and thereby enhance the cohesiveness of the trade union movement in Western Europe.

NOTES

1. *Affiliation* means that members of an organisation pay fees, have the right to vote on policies and organisational changes and are bound by decisions of that organisation (as long as they do not violate the statute of the affiliate). In contrast, *association* in this paper entails limited participation in the controlling bodies. Related to a certain organisation, it implies even less participation or formal and binding elements between the two parties.

2. Unique and against WCL statutory provisions, the Spanish Basque trade union, STV, is a member of both the ICFTU and WCL.

3. See *Report of the Eleventh World Congress of the ICFTU*, Brussels, Belgium, 1977, pp. 26–27.

4. See John P. Windmuller, 'European Regionalism: a new factor in international labour', *Industrial Relations Journal*, Summer Vol. 7, No. 2 (1976), p. 46.

5. Concerning the Resolution for the renewal of world trade unionism of the WCL, the CFDT was not satisfied and felt that the text did not meet the conditions it had laid down for continued affiliation to the WCL (self-governing trade unionism, transformation of the WCL into a trade union research and co-ordination centre, elimination of the international professional federations). Upon having its amendment defeated, the CFDT declared its secession from the WCL. See *Trade Union Information 9/1977*, European Communities (DGX Information), Brussels, pp. 10–12. See also *Report* of the Eleventh World Congress of the ICFTU, p. 54.

6. There are indications that the CNV plans to abandon WCL membership if no progress is made in the relations between the ICFTU and WCL. This could isolate the Belgian CSC, as the sole relatively large European organisation belonging to the WCL, and thus might motivate them to leave as well.

7. While the preamble of the ETUC Constitution speaks of its founding members as "adhering unreservedly to the principles of free and democratic trade unionism," Article 2 of the Constitution omits the word "'free" and states that "applications for membership made by democratic trade union confederations will be considered by the Executive Committee." *ETUC Constitution*, April 1976.

8. For an excellent presentation on the background of CGIL admission to the ETUC, as contrasted with the CGT application, see Windmuller, pp. 41–45.

9. The Third ETUC Congress in Munich charged the Executive Committee with establishing criteria of affiliation and deciding on application demands within one year. See *Intersocial*, May 1979, no. 49. p. 26.

10. See Emil J. Kirchner, *Trade Unions as a Pressure Group in the European Community*, Saxon House, Farnborough, Hants., 1977, p. 166. CGT-FO has indicated that its allegiance is first to the ICFTU and, second, to the ETUC.
11. See Windmuller, p. 45.
12. Wim Kok quoted in *Intersocial*, no. 49, May 1979, p. 28.
13. Windmuller hints that a lessening of financial contributions and thus a certain detachment of ETUC affiliates from the more ephemeral and more frustrating problems of the world-wide body is unavoidable. See Windmuller, p. 47.
14. See Norris Willatt, *Multinational Unions*, Financial Times. London, 1974, p. 60.
15. See Windmuller, p. 38.
16. As stressed in a letter by Charles Levinson, Secretary-General of the International Federation of Chemical and Joint Workers Union (ICF), the important point is that collaboration with the ICFTU is entirely voluntary and is not decreed by statutory obligations of any kind. See *Intersocial*, no. 45, January 1979, p. 25.
17. See *Report* on the Eleventh World Congress of the ICFTU, October 1975, p. 204.
18. See Wolfgang Daubler, "Gewerkschaftsstrategie und Tarifpolitik gegenueber Multinationalen Unternehmen," *Recht der Arbeit*, February 1973, p. 11.
19. See B. C. Roberts, 'Multinational Collective Bargaining: a European Prospect?', *British Journal of Industrial Relations*, 11, no. 1, (March 1973), p. 18; Duane Kujawa, 'Transnational Industrial Relations: a Collective Bargaining Prospect?', in Duane Kujawa (ed.) *International Labor and the Multinational Enterprise* (Praeger: New York, N.Y., 1975), p. 126; and Windmuller, p. 47.
20. Only the EMF has had any success in arranging meetings with the top management of multinational corporations, such as Philips, Fokker-VFW, Brown Boveri and Europemballage, which have their headquarters and main activities in the EC. The EMF stated in its Activity Report that after several years of negative attitude on the part of the employers' organisations in the metal industry (WEM), which prevented the EMF from establishing a permanent committee with this organisation, the EMF succeeded in arranging a meeting between a delegation of the EMF and WEM in November 1975. None of the other European industrial trade union committees has had more success. See *EMF Activity Report* (1974–1977), pp. 118–120.
21. See Kirchner, pp. 168–179. Ruttenberg believes, for example, that national economic social and political environments will shape the goals and needs of local work forces in different ways, making workers and their unions especially vulnerable to the tactics of the multinationals. See Stanley H. Ruttenberg, 'The Union View of Multinationals: An Iterpretation', in R. J. Flanagan and A. R. Weber (eds). *Bargaining without Boundaries* (Chicago: The University of Chicago Press, 1974), p. 189.
22. See Charles Levinson, *International Trade Unionism* (London: George Allen & Unwin, 1972); Duane Kujawa, 'Transnational Industrial Relations' in Duane Kujawa (ed.), *op. cit*. pp. 94–137.
23. For details on 'company councils' and 'industry councils' of the ITS, see Willatt, pp. 23–25.
24. For further details, see Guenter Koepke, 'Union Responses in Continental Europe', in Flanagan and Weber (eds.), *Bargaining without Boundaries*, p. 218. Among those opposed are the three Italian trade unions, the Belgian FGTB and the French CFDT. In its latest action programme the ETUC lists democratisation of the economy as the fourth priority by stating: the ETUC wants to ensure that workers and their representatives have a decisive influence at all levels of economic life. However, it recognises that democratisation takes various forms according to country and that is why it will back affiliated organisations in their efforts to develop and improve methods for democratising the economy. See *General Resolution*, ETUC—3rd Statutory Congress, Munich, 14–18 May 1979.
25. See Kujawa, p. 157.
26. Quoted in *Intersocial*, no. 49, May 1979, p. 29.
27. The Standing Committee on Employment of the EC has an identical structure and similarly lacks binding powers. Both the Standing Committee and the Tripartite Conference on Employment have consultative rather than deliberative roles. The ILO's standards are in the form of model provisions designed as guidelines for enactment through national legislation or practice. But these standards do not constitute

anything like an international jurisdiction administered by an international authority to which multinational corporations could be made accountable.

28. An ILO publication concluded in 1977 that "so far tripartite consultation had achieved little more than a certain degree of verbal consensus among the parties concerned without attaining the series of goals that had been set, particularly regarding reduction of unemployment." *Social and Labour Bulletin,* No. 4 (December 1977), p. 352.

29. See *Intersocial,* no. 49, May 1979, p. 25.

30. See Emil J. Kirchner, 'Interest Group Behaviour at Community Level', in Leon Hurwitz (ed.) *Contemporary Perspectives of EEC Integration,* (Greenwood Press, forthcoming). While the harmonisation record is generally disappointing two directives passed by the EC cover provisions for collective redundancies and safeguards for acquired national trade union rights in cases of mergers of firms. For details on social policy harmonisation at Community level, see Emil J. Kirchner, *Trade Unions as a Pressure Group in the European Community,* pp. 120–122, 150–151, and 171–172.

31. See Windmuller, pp, 47–48.

32. Co-operation with industry committees is encouraged by the ETUC. For example, Wim Kok stated at the Munich Congress that if the ETUC wishes to act on the ground, to sign collective bargaining agreements and to make itself better known to the workers, European industry committees must be developed to become the cornerstone of the trade union movement. See *Intersocial,* no. 49, May 1979, p. 27.

33. Already, the ETUC and some of the European industry committees are concerned over the apparent readiness with which multinational corporations from the capitalist world are setting up operations in the communist countries. See Willatt, pp. 12 and 43–45.

34. One is the Saar-Lorraine-Luxembourg Inter-regional Trade Union Council, the other is the Meuse-Rhine Inter-regional Trade Union Council, representing over 600,000 affiliated workers. The former has as its administrative bodies a joint conference, a bureau and a permanent secretariat.